Praise For *Forever Upward*

Forever Upward comes at
refreshed and reminded of
The book is filled with "the
well as stronger meat to urg
are encouraged to set our ey
Everyone should remember, ...ayer never fails; we just fail to
pray!"

Jim and Carolyn Munsey
Founders and Senior Pastors
New Life Family Church
Suburban Atlanta

Suellen has captured the heart of our Father God as she pours
out her wisdom and shares the truths that have shaped her life
– especially the truth that "all your children shall be blessed."
You will be strengthened and encouraged as you share her
journey captivated in *Forever Upward.*

Bobbie Jean Merck, Founder and President
A Great Love International Ministries
Toccoa, Georgia

I would like to get on a platform with a megaphone and say,
"Attention, mothers: if you have lost your hope, this book is
for you!" *Forever Upward* will bring you hope and build your
faith as you pursue God's answers for your children.

Sheryl Smith
Wife of Evangelist, Jarvis Smith
Blue Mountain, Mississippi

Forever Upward is a book which is needed in the body of Christ.

Germaine Copeland, Founder and President
Word Ministries
Roswell, Georgia
Best-Selling Author, *Prayers That Avail Much*

Forever Upward

*A Mother's Journey
Through Prayer*

Suellen Estes

Hutchins House
Blue Mountain, Mississippi

Unless otherwise identified
Scripture quotations are taken from
the New American Standard Bible®
Copyright© 1960,1962,1963,1968,1971,1972,1973,
1975,1977, 1995
by the Lockman Foundation
used by permission (www.Lockman.org)

Cover design by Mickey Estes Photography

ISBN-13: 978-0-615-33477-6
LCCN: 2010902300

ATTN: Quantity discounts are available to your church,
educational institution, or organization
for re-selling, educational purposes, gifts, or fundraising.
For more information, please contact the publisher

Hutchins House Publishing Company LLC
Blue Mountain, Mississippi 38610
www.foreverupward.com
publisher@foreverupward.com

*I dedicate this book to
my Wonderful Family*

My husband, Mickey

*My children and grandchildren
Adrienne and Bob*
*Caroline, Lauren, Natalie,
Victoria, and Stephanie*

Leslie and Tom
John Christian, Briggs, and Charlie

Libby and Jon
Griffin

John and Stephany

You bring me such great joy!

Acknowledgements

I want to express a sincere thank you to those who helped lay the foundations of faith in my life:

Griffin and Jennie Wheless, my parents
Their Christian example was unsurpassed. I know they are cheering me on from Heaven right now.

George Wheless, my brother
He is in that cloud of witnesses also - and probably cracking a few jokes.

During those early days in Atlanta, some wonderful teachers helped open my eyes to a deeper walk:

Jim and Carolyn Munsey
After my encounter with Jesus in 1979, you were the first to lay a foundation of faith which is still with me today. Carolyn, I can still hear your voice as you taught.

Germaine Copeland
Bobbie Jean Merck
During those early days as you ministered, I sat in the middle of the crowd and soaked up every word. You powerful women of God inspired me so significantly.

I also want to thank those who helped me with this book:

Mickey
You have been with me in every aspect of this endeavor. Your ideas and your talents have made this possible.

Adrienne, Leslie, Libby, John, Stephany, and my sister, Ruthie
Thanks for all your editing, ideas, and support.

Life Connection Church
I am very grateful for your encouragement and your patience as I worked on this project.

Table of Contents

Introduction

Have you ever felt overwhelmed by the needs of your family? I have! In April of 2006 I began writing this book. By that time I had spent many years studying God's Word, letting Him teach me about prayer according to His Word. I had always spent a good deal of time directing that prayer toward the needs of my children and there had been many victories.

Little did I know that the worst battles were yet to come. Suddenly our world seemed to be turned upside down. Forces beyond belief were coming against our children. I stopped writing the book and we began the greatest battle of our lives.

War is messy. Our battle plans seldom are executed with perfect precision, and we often find ourselves in confusion when we are facing a crisis. However, God's battle plan is perfect. When we are going through the greatest dilemmas, if we stay close to our Father and His Word, we will see His power lift us up above the fray.

As a result of these trials, I stand here today humbler, yet stronger. I am stronger because my strength doesn't come from my own abilities – MY faith, MY knowledge of the Word, MY spirituality. My strength comes from my Lord. Over the last few years, I have felt very weak at times. However, God's power is perfected in my weakness. (II Corinthians 12:9)

Because of these experiences, I can speak with greater assurance than ever. I can also speak with greater understanding of God's principles – mercy, forgiveness, and perseverance. He is truly faithful. I will forever praise Him for being with us in trouble. He has delivered us as only He can do.

Life is a journey. Often times I have played a special game with my grandchildren. There is a path which is loaded with pitfalls and pleasant surprises. As you roll the dice, you may receive extra advantages or you may fall into a pit.

Sometimes life can seem like that. We think everything is going well and then we can find ourselves in a sand trap! As long as we are on this earth, we need to stay alert to the obstacles. As prayer warriors for our families and friends we must watch. If we will do that, we know that God always has the answers we need. He will lead us, comfort us, correct us, and carry us to higher places on His mountain. The greatest sorrows can become our greatest victories.

Over the years I have encountered many mothers in crisis. I have come to learn that within the heart of every born again mother, there lies a longing for the welfare of her children. This longing is put there by God Himself. It is evidence of the call that is on her life to protect and care for her offspring. It is also evidence of God's desire for her to pray for her own. This longing, this desire, this call will propel a mother to rise early, spend many hours with her Father God and His Word, and spend hours praying for her children. This call will also compel that mother never to give up.

This book is written to such mothers. In it you will find stories of mothers just like you. They have raised their children to the best that they knew. Did they make mistakes? Of course they did! No one is perfect. Some of them even made lots of mistakes before coming to the Lord. They were worldly and self-centered. Yet when they came to the knowledge of the Lord Jesus and saw Him for who He truly is, they turned to Him and His promises. They repented, they asked for forgiveness, and they forgave others. A new day dawned in their hearts and they reached out for the wonderful, miraculous life God had for them. As they laid hold of what their Father had in store for them, they saw transformation in the lives of their children also.

I have changed the names of people for the sake of privacy, yet all of the real life examples scattered throughout the book happened to people I knew. People just like you.

My prayer for you is that as we share in the coming pages, you will be uplifted. God has miracles waiting for you also. Reach out to Him. Reach out to His power. Reach out to His promises. Let faith arise in your heart. Receive the miracles your Father has for YOU. There is nothing too difficult for our God.

Let us let Him lead us Forever Upward!

First Words

An evangelist's wayward daughter mocked and ridiculed her father for many years. It seemed that she would never change. One night, as she was partying at a motel, she suddenly "came to her senses." Weeping and broken, she called her dad, repented, and has been in ministry with him ever since.

A Christian's grandson was hooked on heroin. He was sent to prison, but as soon as he was free, he returned to the habit. For several years the young man was in and out of prison. One night the grandson had a terrible car wreck and was thrown into a ditch by a lonely road. In a semi-conscious state, the man remembered the words of his godly grandfather and gave his life to the Lord. The rescue and quick recovery were miraculous. That was many years ago, and he has remained faithful to this day.

A husband and wife who had recently committed their

lives to the Lord, were devastated when they realized that their teenage sons were hooked on drugs. The boys were entrenched in a harmful lifestyle which they financed by illegal activity. The two sons eventually went to prison. However, while in prison, they were both radically saved and delivered. Upon release, one of the boys entered the ministry.

What do these stories have in common? PRAYER. In every case, the parent or grandparent was persistent in praying for his or her children. Circumstances may have looked impossible and there may have been delays, but the answer came in every case! Nothing is impossible with God!

Whatever your situation, God has the answer. As we share His plan and purpose in the pages ahead, know that He loves you and your children. Their well-being is His will. Their deliverance is His will. Whatever your need, He can provide it.

We are about to start on a journey – a journey of hope; a journey of deliverance. We will learn why we pray, how to pray, and what to pray. As we continue the journey, we will know our Father better and hear His voice with greater clarity. We will also have a greater hope and faith as we live this life with Him

As you proceed with the book, let me encourage you to read every scripture mentioned and take some time letting God speak to you. You might want to make lots of notes. I hope you enjoy the journey. Life can be full of adventure and excitement if we follow the path He has for us!

And he will be
like a tree
firmly planted
by streams of water,
which yields its fruit in
its season
Psalm 1:3

Chapter One
Living Water Flows

Harvey and June Lancet had a dramatice salvation experience when June was healed from cancer. She had been diagnosed with breast cancer - in a fairly advanced stage. In desperation, the couple attended a healing service at a local church and her cancer disappeared.

Both of the Lancets, jubilant from the experience, committed their lives to the Lord, and thus began a transformation. They began attending church regularly and studying the Bible daily. Life was so much better.

There was only one problem - or should we say two? Ken and Martin, their two teenage sons were hooked on drugs. As their habits were increasing in intensity, so were their monetary demands. So the two young men began robbing stores to finance their habits. Harvey and June knew that they had not raised their sons to live responsible lives. Yet they had seen

God's glorious hand in their own lives. They knew that He was a merciful God, and they were counting on that mercy!

As the parents were growing in their knowledge of God's Word and in faith, they began to pray the Word back to God and to speak it about their sons. No matter what happened, they prayed and prophesied (spoke) God's Word.

June told me that the turning point for her faith in what they were doing was when she saw in the Bible a word about the thief.

> Proverb 6:31
> *When the thief gets caught, he must repay seven times.*

At that moment of discovery, June decided that since the devil had stolen from her sons, he owed them back seven times what he had stolen. June began to pray this proverb back to God and to speak it out loud into the atmosphere. Harvey was praying and speaking his own decree that, "All of his sons were disciples taught of the Lord." (Isaiah 54:13) They determined in their hearts that they would never give up.

Well, even with all the prayer, the downhill skid continued for Ken and Martin. While in their late teens they both were arrested for robbery and sentenced to the state penitentiary. At that time, many parents would have given up. They would have said that the boys had reached the point of no return. They would have decided that there was no hope. Not the Lancets! They dug in their heels even harder. They knew what God's Word said, and they would not be denied!

Several years passed and I lost contact with the Lancets. One day I happened to see June at the mall. She was glowing! Ken and Martin had just been released from prison. While in prison they both had committed their lives to the Lord. One of them was even going into full time evangelism. Wow!

When you hear a story like this, what comes to your mind? Do you wonder how the Lancets acquired the faith to continue their prayers? Do you marvel at their tenacity? Do you wonder why they were praying the Word of God? Do you wonder how they were so sure of God's will? All of these questions are quite common when people encounter dramatic turnarounds. These are the kinds of questions we want to answer in this book.

Now let's turn the attention to you and your children. What's the status with your children: are you satisfied with their Christian walk, or do you have concerns about it? Do they seem to be drawn to people who build them up, or to those who tear them down? Do you have great confidence that your prayers for your children will be answered? Do you understand why we pray or how to pray? Do you feel overwhelmed with the responsibility of raising your children to be productive Christians? Do you battle fear when you see all of the evil in the society around them?

If these questions strike a chord with you, then read on. This book was written for you. This book was written for the purpose of helping people to understand how and why we pray, how we can know God's will, and how we increase our faith. Your Creator wants to show you His plan for prayer and what it can accomplish. He wants to increase your faith and your knowledge of Him.

As we proceed, I am going to share with you many of my personal experiences with the Lord. For more than thirty years, He has been the source of my strength. But it hasn't always been that way. In my early adult life, I took a detour which brought me a lot of pain. As I share with you some of my discoveries as my life turned around, I hope you will be encouraged in your walk with Him.

Many years ago, as I was reading the Bible, I came across a passage which resounded in my spirit. As you walk with the Lord, He will bring scriptures to you which will become foundational stones in building your belief system. This passage was such a stone for me. Even though I was a relatively new believer, I knew that this stone would be significant to me forever. It seemed to bring such clarity as to why Christians don't always see things the same way. I want to share this very special scripture with you.

In the following passage Ezekiel tells of a vision he had. An angel showed him God's holy temple. From the altar, water was flowing out into the land around. The water represented the Holy Spirit of God. As the angel and Ezekiel waded out into the stream, there were some wonderful life lessons. Look with me.

Ezekiel 47:1-12

Then he brought me back to the door of the house; and behold, water was flowing from under the threshold of the house toward the east, for the house faced east. And the water was flowing down from under, from the right side of the house, from south of the altar.

And he brought me out by way of the north gate and led me around on the outside to the outer gate by way of the gate that faces east. And behold, water was trickling from the south side.

When the man went out toward the east with a line in his hand, he measured a thousand cubits, and he led me through the water, water reaching the ankles.

Again he measured a thousand and led me through the water, water reaching the knees. Again he measured a thousand and led me through the water, water reaching the loins.

Again he measured a thousand; and it was a river that I could not ford, for the water had risen, enough water to swim in, a river that could not be forded.

And he said to me, "Son of Man, have you seen this?" Then he brought me back to the bank of the river.

Now when I had returned, behold, on the bank of the river there were very many trees on the one side and on the other.

Then he said to me, "These waters go out toward the eastern region and go down into the Arabah; then they go toward the sea, being made to flow into the sea, and the waters of the sea become fresh.

And it will come about that every living creature which swarms in every place where the river goes, will live. And there will be very many fish, for these waters go there, and the others become fresh; so everything will live where the river goes.

And it will come about that fishermen will stand beside it; from Engedi to Eneglaim there will be a place for the spreading of nets. Their fish will be according to their kinds, like the fish of the Great Sea, very many.

But its swamps and marshes will not become fresh; they will be left for salt.

And by the river on its bank, on one side and on the other, will grow all kinds of trees for food. Their leaves will not wither, and their fruit will not fail. They will bear every month because their water flows from the sanctuary, and their fruit will be for food and their leaves for healing.

Here, Ezekiel has a vision of an angel showing him a profound spiritual truth. The water represents the Holy Spirit of God flowing from His altar in Heaven. He then shows how the people of God walk into the water. First they go into the water up to their ankles, then their knees, their loins, and finally over their heads. Then the angel makes it clear that only the "water where you swim," the water over your head, is the water of healing. On the banks of the "water where you swim," are trees bearing fruit in every season. (You will find a similar picture in Revelation 22:1-2). The shallow water is only for marsh. Nothing can live there.

As I read this passage, I saw a picture of many people wading out toward a great powerful river. Many were standing in water up to their ankles. They acknowledged God and considered themselves Christians, but they had little desire to know Him better or to walk with Him closely. They wanted "their space." As the water got deeper, the numbers of waders decreased. As I looked toward the river, I noticed that the numbers were very few. Most people were too busy to spend much time or energy seeking their God. Only a few were out in the deep water where they could experience the deepest life their Father had to offer.

Only a few were out in the deep water where they could experience the deepest life their Father had to offer

---

I knew where I had been all of my life. I had been standing in ankle deep water. I had wanted God's blessings for myself and my family, yet I had neither taken the time nor expended the energy to have a deep walk with Him. In fact, I didn't even know about such a thing. So there I stood with my feet wet, but with little power, little understanding, and little fruit in my life.

That was beginning to change. As I sat there with my heart lifted to Him, I felt despair washing away and hope rising within me. I knew that I was connected to my Maker, and I knew that He had a great plan for me and for my children. I also knew that He had all the answers I needed as I moved down life's path.

What does all of this have to do with praying for your children? Everything! Many people are praying desperate prayers while standing in ankle deep water. Maybe their own lives are not committed to God. Or maybe they don't understand His will or His ways. It could be that they don't understand how prayer works or why we pray. Whatever the reason, they don't know what they are doing to hinder God's work in their lives. They are just "hoping and praying" (which is code for "whining and crying") and getting more discouraged all of the time.

I want more than that. Don't you? I want to know the deepest secrets of our Father. I want to know how His kingdom works and I know that you do, too. So I would like to share with you some of the lessons I have learned over the last 30 years of walking with the Lord.

I am reminded of a story about a great evangelist who was preaching to a crowd during the late 1800's. He said, "The world has yet to see what God can do with a man whose life is totally committed to Him." Standing in the back of the room was a young lawyer named Charles Finney. His heart was pricked and he said, "I want to be that man." On that day Finney made a total commitment to Jesus and eventually became the greatest evangelist America has ever known. There were reports of entire villages coming to the Lord as a result of his crusades.

You might be thinking, "Well I am not called to be a great evangelist." Maybe not, but God's desire is to have every believer have a close walk with Him. He is ready and waiting – standing at the door and knocking- wanting to be more of a part of our lives. The choice to let Him in is ours. He has so many pleasant surprises for those who desire Him also.

As you proceed through this book, I pray that you will come into greater understanding and greater hope. You will start walking out into deeper water - the water where you swim. As you do that, God's light will become brighter and brighter. Faith will arise in your heart. You will begin to see- first in your spirit, then in the natural, the answers to your prayers. The blessings will begin to flow out in greater abundance. Our God is faithful!

In the next chapters we will be answering many questions. We will lay a foundation of knowing God and understanding His kingdom that will bring us to a new level of prayer. When we understand God's kingdom plan for prayer we will soar with our faith. Our prayers will have zeal and answers will follow. Deliverance will come to us and our children.

Be patient as we proceed. We may cover some ground that seems unnecessary to you. However, if you will continue with me, you will be enriched in your understanding and you will also be enriched in your ability to pray.

Section One

...and he led me
into
the water ,
water reaching
the ankles

*For God
so loved the world
that he gave
His only begotten Son
that whoever believes in
Him should not perish,
but have eternal life
John 3:16*

Chapter Two
Encounter
With Jesus

We don't want to stay in ankle deep water, but we have to start there. Can you recall a time at the beach? If so, you'll remember the trip out into the deep water. When you are wading from a beach out into deep water, you have to start in the shallows. Your feet get securely planted and then you are ready to walk out deeper. If you try to run out too quickly, you'll lose your footing and fall. We need to use that principle now. So let's take it the way God gives it to us – one step at a time.

For us to understand our place in prayer we have to have our eyes opened to spiritual things. This only comes when we are born again children of God.

John 3:3

Jesus said, "Truly, truly I say to you, unless one is born again, he cannot see the kingdom of God."

Let's think for a minute about what this means. There is a huge difference between being a born again Christian and being a disciple of any other religion. Other religions have rules and principles which are supposed to bring people to perfection. Yet rules and principles will never change your nature. If you are truly a born again Christian, your nature is changed.

It works like this: when you honestly accept the cross of Jesus as the sacrifice for your sins, you are forgiven and cleansed. Then your spirit - the Bible refers to it as the "inner man" (Ephesians 3:16) or the "hidden person of the heart,"(I Peter 3:4) comes alive. You become a new person. The Holy Spirit comes to reside within your spirit - leading you, instructing you, and empowering you. God's life is now within you.

John 3:16

For God so loved the world that He gave His only begotten Son, that whosoever should believe in Him should not perish, but have everlasting life.

When we hear this verse, we often think that "everlasting life" or "eternal life" simply means that we will live forever. It's true that it does mean we will live forever, but there is more to it than that. The Greek word in the original text is "zoe." Zoe is a very significant word which means "God's life." If we have God's life, we will live eternally, but also His life is on the inside of us right now. He is bringing us insight and empowerment to live every day.

It took me many years to learn this. I grew up in a godly home with wonderful Christian parents. As a child, my desire was to commune with the Lord and have a life committed to Him. However, as I grew into adulthood my path turned. During my early adult years, I wanted to be a "good person," but I took the wrong approach. Intellectualism was king. Think. Think. Think. Reason. Reason. Reason.

Analysis and reason have their place in our thought processes - they are wonderful gifts from God. In fact, when we are living as God desires, we will be exercising these gifts to their fullest capacity. Yet our intellect can never be our approach to God. Nevertheless that's exactly how I was trying to approach Him, and clearly I was having very little success. Our Creator is too great and too all-knowing for us to find Him with our finite minds. He is Spirit, and we communicate with Him through our spirits —not just our minds.

For several years I thought my theories were reasonable and effective. I read a wide variety of books from many different religions and thought I was finding "truth" throughout. Although I considered myself a Christian, I thought there were many paths to God - not understanding the sacrifice of Jesus. In fact, I even wondered why Jesus had died on the cross. I didn't understand it.

During those early years, I prided myself on staying current with all the latest books and topics to enhance my active social life. A bigger house, a more sophisticated neighborhood: these were the things I sought. I wanted my three children to have the best that money could buy - the best schools, the best vacations, and all the experiences which would go with that lifestyle. Though I considered myself a Christian, worldliness prevailed in my heart - and worldliness would eventually bring me down!

After about thirteen years of these pursuits, some major pitfalls appeared and my life caved in. All of my erratic "seeking" was like dust in my hands. I knew I needed a power greater than myself to lift me up, but that power didn't seem to be available. My heart was like a vacuum. My prideful lifestyle had been exposed for what it was – emptiness.

The year was 1979 and my life was in total chaos. A couple of years before, I had gone through a hurtful divorce and I was overwhelmed with loneliness, shame, and feelings of failure. I had a tremendous love for my three children and wanted the best for them, yet I felt completely inadequate as I tried to provide their needs financially as well as emotionally. On top of everything else, I was using several nightly glasses of wine to "cope." I was heartbroken and desperate.

Finally, getting to the end of my pride, I fell face down on the kitchen floor of my home and "turned myself in." Surrendering to the Lord, my prayer was not conventional. In a moment of desperation, I cried out, "Jesus, if you are real, I need you and I want you!" As I waited in

---

For the first time in my adult life, I was aware of the reality of God's love for me personally

---

the silence, an amazing peace enveloped me. It was as if a voice were saying, "I Am, and I want you too!" A phenomenal transformation began.

As I felt God's mercy pour down upon me like liquid love, I knew that something very powerful was happening to me. Moments before, despair had engulfed me; now joy was bubbling up from deep within. There had been incredible loneliness, but no longer. I knew I was connected to my Maker. I was no longer alone.

II Corinthians 5:17, 18

Therefore if any man is in Christ, he is a new creature; the old things are passed away; behold new things have come. Now all these new things are from God.

That reality was exploding within me. Deep within my heart I knew that my sins had been forgiven - and that I was starting a new life with God's mercy and empowerment.

It was amazing! Never in all of my reasoning had I understood the simplicity of the Gospel. I always tried to complicate things, yet this was so simple. I simply told Jesus that I wanted to be His. He accepted me, and I was entering into a life of freedom. How did I know? Deep within my spirit, I just knew! I knew that my sins were forgiven. I felt so clean and pure; so full of life. For the first time in my adult life, I was aware of the reality of God's goodness and His love for me personally, as well as His love for my children. Just basking in that love made my faith rise. Certainly His plans for us were good ones, filled with joy and satisfaction.

My eyes were opened to begin to see God's plan like never before. It was as if the world had always been black and white and had just burst into brilliant color. Life was good; better than it had ever been. The best part was that I was beginning to have a relationship, indeed a friendship with the Lord.

In the days that followed, I explored God's Word in a new way. Hidden treasures seemed to leap off the pages - treasures which would help me to understand life and live it more successfully. Every day became an adventure!

Up until that time, I had admired Jesus as a "good man." I had loved the Bible stories of His compassion and forgiveness toward the sinners. Now I received His compassion and forgiveness for me and my children. I had loved the stories of healing and deliverance as He walked the earth. Now I saw His desire to heal and deliver me from all of the forces which had almost crushed me. It was amazing!

Now, how about you? Have you received Jesus as your Lord and Savior? Have you committed your life to Him? Have you asked Him to live in your heart? Have you "turned yourself in?"

That's your starting point, just as it was mine. We

may think we are too good or too smart for something so simple. But we are not. The amazing thing about our just God is that a person growing up in a primitive village in Africa has the same ability to approach Him as we do. Our approach to Him is not because of our own goodness or our achievements or our grasp of intellectual integrity. We just have to receive Jesus on faith and recognize our limited ability. That humility is the golden key which opens the door into the heavenlies.

When you are delving into God's special plans for prayer, you must start with your heart and life belonging to Him. It's the best decision you will ever make. And indeed it IS a decision. He's ready. Are you?

After our commitment to Him, we want to take some time to concentrate on His love for us as individuals. Our God is good - full of love and mercy. Don't think of that love as just a "generic" love for everyone. Think of His love for you personally. He is a personal, one-on-one God, and He is bringing us abundant life as we continue with Him. He is always for us - bringing us into a blessed life. When we fall into trouble or make mistakes, He is the one who helps us to climb out and try again, always empowering us to do better next time.

James 1:16,17

Do not be deceived, my beloved brethren. Every good thing bestowed and every perfect gift is from above, coming down from the Father of lights, with whom there is no variation, or shifting shadow.

He doesn't vary His plan from good to bad. All good is from Him, and He never varies in that.

John 10:10

The thief comes only to steal, and kill, and destroy; I came that they might have life, and might have it abundantly.

There is a thief here (the devil) who tries to bring you harm. God only brings good, abundant life.

Jeremiah 33:11
*Give thanks to the Lord of hosts
For the Lord is good.*

God is always good.

John 3:16,17
*For God so loved the world, that He gave His only begotten Son, that whoever believes in Him should not perish, but have everlasting life.
For God did not send the Son into the world to judge*

the world, but that the world should be saved through
Him.

So where does all that destruction come from? It comes from the devil, Satan, the enemy of your soul. Right now, let's concentrate on how much our God loves us. His desire is for us is to recognize that love and to know that He wants us to have a blessed, successful life. He wants to visit with us everyday – to have conversation with us. He wants us to take all of our problems to Him and let Him share His answers. Out of our hearts of love toward Him, we praise and bless Him and He blesses us. It's a love relationship.

This is where our prayer starts. We start by spending time with our Father – everyday. We talk to Him; He talks to us. In His presence we see clearly and our faith rises. We know that our God is on our side. His love for us is always there, never-ending, full of wisdom, favor, and empowerment.

In His presence, we see clearly and our faith rises

Now take some time to think of people you know

from the many facets of your life. What a variety, wouldn't you say? Some are good in music or art. Some are accomplished in mathematics and reasoning. There are those great in sports; others excel in organization. Some seem to have a knack for communicating with other people. Everyone is good at something! What is important here is to realize that God created each person as a unique individual. They are not like "foot soldiers" in a video game. They are all different.

Now take some time to think about yourself as God's creation. You are special - an individual. When you begin to see yourself, not just as a ho-hum person, but God's very handiwork, your confidence rises. You stop comparing yourself with others, and start appreciating who you are. As you do that, you truly begin to receive your Father's love for YOU.

The same goes for your children. Each has been created as God desires, with individuality only He could imagine. And along with the unique gifting, there is a unique plan for each one - a good plan, which unfolds as we continue to walk with Him.

Now, back to my story...From the night that I comitted my life to the Lord, I have experienced His goodness. He immediately began to draw my daughters closer to Him. We found a church fellowship, full of loving people who helped us come to know Him better. Then, a few years later, He brought to me a wonderful husband, Mickey, and gave us a son to go with our three daughters. He eventually called us into the ministry.

It would take several volumes to talk about all the blessings he has brought our way. Have there been disappointments? Of course there have been! But God has always been faithful to heal and restore and get us back into the game.

One morning a few years ago, I had a pleasant surprise from the Lord. Just as I was awaking, I heard His voice say, "You are my favorite." Well, we all know that the Lord loves us all, so I knew that I wasn't really His "favorite." Then He reminded me of some scriptures in John's gospel - some verses which have encouraged me many times. John three times referred to himself as "the disciple whom Jesus loved." (John 21:7, 20, 24). Isn't that compelling? He received the love of Jesus so completely that he felt as if he were the one whom Jesus loved the most. That's the way the Lord wants it to be. He wants each one of us to feel like He loves us the most. Such an incredible power enters our lives when we receive His love so completely.

You also are one of His favorites! Receive from Him daily. He is your best friend. The time you spend with your Creator

---

You are one of His favorites

---

is the most important time you will spend on earth. Talk to Him. Listen to Him and obey Him. He is better than you think!

Let's Go Deeper

1. Read Jeremiah 29:11

As you pray and meditate on this scripture, let the Lord show you some plans He has for you.

2. Read James 1:16, 17 and John 10:10

Meditate on the scriptures in this chapter. Write down some times when you have blamed God for hurtful things in your life. Be honest. He knows it all anyway. Take those things to Him in prayer and allow Him to show you the truth in the light of these scriptures.

3. Write a paragraph about God's goodness in your life. Think about the times He saved you from dangerous situations. Instead of listing all the problems you have had, list all the blessings you have received.

Thy Word
is a lamp
to my feet
and a light
to my path
Psalm 119:105

Chapter Three
Just What
Is God's Word?

When our lives belong to God, we pray for many reasons. Of course we praise Him. We thank Him. We commit to Him. Sometimes we just "hang out" with him. We ask for direction and strength. We also pray for God to change the lives of our families when we see them going astray. These are called "intercessory" prayers and they are very special to us and to God. They also can be very productive if they are prayed according to God's plan. So where can we find God's plan? A significant encounter with God gave me some understanding.

In January 1981 I had a life-changing experience with the Holy Spirit. One Monday night I was almost asleep when I was suddenly jolted back to consciousness. At the time, some Iranian rebels (now the present rulers) had overthrown the government. They had seized the American Embassy and were holding American workers hostage. For more than a year these people were held captive, and our government was not able to obtain their release. It was a very tense time for everyone involved.

My Father, the Creator of the Universe, the One who knows all mysteries and all knowledge, has sent this message to us for our deliverance

---

That winter night the Holy Spirit awoke me with an almost audible voice, "What if you could send a coded message to the hostages in Iran? It would be a plan for escape – a perfect plan! The message would be understood by the captives, but the guards would not be able to decipher the code, so they couldn't stop it." Of course I said, "That would be great!" However, I was very curious about such an inquiry. This seemed like such a strange question, yet I recognized the voice of the Lord. Then the bombshell: "That is what I have done through My Word. The whole world is held captive by the evil one. I have sent a coded message to My people. If they read the message and allow the Holy Spirit to show them the truth within it, they will have their plan of escape. The enemy doesn't understand My Word or My plan. If you will allow My Spirit to show it to you, you will be free and help others to become free also."

By that time, I was fully awake and praising My Father. Then came another jolt. "What if you sent the message to the hostages in Iran, and they didn't recognize it for what it was? What if they tossed it aside and didn't bother to read it?" I knew what was coming next. "That's what people have done with My Word."

Now wide awake, I went into the den and sat holding my Bible in my hands. Looking at it, I thought, "What a miracle!" My Father, the Creator of the Universe, the One who knows all mysteries and all knowledge, has sent this message to us for our deliverance. "What a miracle!" I sat there for several hours thanking my Father for His goodness.

In my earlier days, I had thought of myself as an intellectual, but I was not! A true intellectual would have understanding of his Creator and His plans, but I had no such understanding! Dissecting the Bible as if it were just literature written in another time, I had critiqued and explained away so many of the truths. Others had escaped my attention entirely. That night in 1981 my life changed forever as I saw God's Word for what it was: His miraculous communication with His people. As I read it, I began to see more than I had ever seen before. Underlying the Words on the page, I heard My Father speaking to me personally. My hunger for His Word and my revelation of it increased tenfold!

As truth began to unfold, I began to see God's plan for man. Up until that time, God's reasons for putting man on the earth seemed to be foggy to me. I would hear people with many different theories about man's purpose. But I never had a clear cut understanding of it all. That began to change.

God, in His sovereignty, created the "rules of the universe," and He has never changed them

---

God is sovereign. He is Creator of the universe and of us. He is the All-powerful One. He made the rules and He can run the universe any way He wants to. However, He is also stable and unchanging. He doesn't whimsically plan to do things a certain way one day and then change His plan the next. He is an unchanging, orderly God. God, in His sovereignty, created the "rules of the universe," and He hasn't changed them.

As you read through the Bible, you see His purpose unfolding and staying on path. Man has strayed, but God never has. Before man was put on the earth, our Father was faithfully and diligently bringing His purpose to fruition. The devil may have tried to stop it, but of course, the devil could never stop the plan of God. He is no match for our God.

The first rule of the universe is that we must recognize God's Word for what it is. When we don't honor it as God's Word, we can't begin to understand His plans. Some people take it as a history book just telling us what happened many years ago. Even some theologians seem to treat it that way. They will do lots of research about the time, place and culture of the stories – all of which are fine in their place, but there's more! Others treat it as a law book, using the Bible to see what God considers "lawful" and "unlawful." That is not the whole story either. Neither of these vantage points provides the full story.

God's Word is supernatural. It was spoken supernaturally to many different people over hundreds of years. Even though men wrote the words, the truths were divinely inspired. This miraculous book contains secrets: knowledge

God's Word is supernatural

and wisdom which we could not know any other way.

It contains secrets for our abundant living. It contains secrets for our deliverance and secrets to help us bring deliverance to our children, our families, and others around us.

We need more than what man can do for himself. We need God's power and favor operating in our lives. The Bible, God's supernatural book, can truly bring the influence of God into your life and that of your family.

Let's Go Deeper

1. Read Psalm 119

This longest Psalm in the Bible will help you see the importance of God's Word.

2. Try to remember some verses which have spoken to you in years past. Write down some of the things which God spoke to you.

 Were you encouraged?

Did your understanding increase?

*But the one
who sows
to the Spirit
shall
from the Spirit
reap life
Galatians 6:8*

Chapter Four
Farming
With God

D o you want more faith? I do. Even a surface reading of the Bible, shows us that faith is important in prayer. Jesus marveled at the great faith of the centurian (Matthew 8:10), and He rebuked His disciples when they showed lack of faith (Matthew 17:17). In Mark 5:25-34 a woman who had suffered with a "hemorrhage" for twelve years, touched Jesus and received her healing. Jesus said, "Your faith has made you well." When the Syrophoenician woman asked for the Lord to heal her daughter, Jesus said, "O woman, your faith is great, be it done for you as you wish."(Matthew 15:28)

Okay, we know that we need faith. But how do we get it? Many years ago, one of my daughters prayed with a friend to receive Jesus. She came home from school really excited. In leading Joe to the Lord, she had asked him if he believed in his heart that Jesus was raised from the dead. He closed his eyes, held his breath, and tensed every muscle in his body as he gasped, "Yes." We are like that, aren't we? We try to believe more, but we really can't make ourselves believe. We either believe or we don't. So can we change that? Yes, if we do it God's way, we can increase our faith in God and His Word? There is a kind of faith which is beyond just acknowledgement. That's the kind of faith we need to have our prayers answered. The next few chapters will help us attain that faith.

We speak of God's Word as supernatural. What do we mean? Webster's Dictionary says the word applies to an "order of existence beyond the visible, observable universe," or "something appearing to transcend the laws of nature." When

---

God's Word operates on a level which is higher than man's ability

---

God intervenes in our lives, we are experiencing the "supernatural." God's Word operates on a level which is higher than man's ability.

When we say that the Word is "supernatural," we refer to several things. First of all it was supernaturally given to men by God, and now He supernaturally reveals it to us. But there is more. As we read God's Word and meditate on it, our spirits grow. We grow in understanding and we also grow in faith.

In Genesis 1, we read of God's creative plan. First He created plants, which have only one part: a body. Then He created animals, which have a body and a soul. (If you have a pet dog, you know that it has emotions. Sometimes it is sad; sometimes it is happy. It also has the ability to learn proper obedience. These elements are part of the soul.) Finally, He created man from the dust and breathed His own breath (His Spirit) into Him. Thus man had three parts: body, soul, and spirit.

Each part of man has different functions and different needs. Our bodies need food to grow, our souls need natural education and natural encouragement to grow, and our spirits need God's Word to grow. If all of our parts are nourished, we will truly fulfill our purpose. Almost everyone knows about the needs of the body and the natural man. However, few people really understand that their spirit NEEDS the food of God's Word.

Jesus said, "The Words I have spoken to you are Spirit and they are life."(John 6:63) He also said, "Man shall not live by bread alone, but by every Word that proceeds out of the mouth of God."(Luke 4:4)

At another time, Jesus introduced the Word as seed and showed how it needs to be planted into the heart of man. Perhaps this is the most famous parable in the Bible: the "Sower sows the Word."

Look with me at Mark 4:3-20 Jesus is talking to His disciples.

> *Listen to this! Behold the sower went out to sow and it came about that as he was sowing, some seed fell beside the road, and the birds came and ate it up.*
>
> *And other seed fell on the rocky ground where it did not have much soil, and immediately it sprang up because it had no depth of soil. And after the sun had risen, it was scorched; and because it had no root, it withered away.*
>
> *And other seed fell among the thorns, and the thorns came up and choked it, and it yielded no crop.*
>
> *And other seeds fell into the good soil and as they grew up and increased, they yielded a crop and produced thirty, sixty, and a hundredfold.*
>
> *And He was saying, "He who has ears to hear, let him hear."*
>
> *And as soon as He was alone, His followers, along with the twelve, began asking Him about the parables.*
>
> *And He was saying to them, "To you has been given the mystery of the kingdom of God, but those who are outside get everything in parables. In order that while seeing, they may see and not perceive; and while hearing, they may hear and not understand lest they return and be forgiven."*

And He said to them, "Do you not understand this parable? And how will you understand all the parables?

The sower sows the word.

And these are the ones who are beside the road where the word is sown; and when they hear, immediately Satan comes and takes away the word which has been sown in them.

And in a similar way these are the ones on whom seed was sown on the rocky places, who, when they hear the word they immediately receive it with joy; And they have no firm root in themselves, but are only temporary; then when affliction or persecution arises because of the word, immediately they fall away.

And others are the ones on whom seed was sown among the thorns; these are the ones who have heard the word and the worries of the world, and the deceitfulness of riches, and desires for other things enter in and choke the word and it becomes unfruitful.

And these are the ones on whom seed was sown on good soil; and they hear the word and accept it, and bear fruit, thirty, sixty, and a hundredfold."

So Jesus compares God's Word to seeds, and He explains several different scenarios. Sometimes the seed produces a lot. Sometimes it produces nothing. Sometimes it starts producing and then hits problems. Is the seed different in each case? No. The seed is the same. What makes the difference? The type of soil makes the difference. And the soil for God's Word is the heart of man. Your heart will make the difference in what you are able to produce. The condition of your heart will determine how you receive God's Word for your spirit.

So how do the hearts differ in the parable? The first heart is hard. The word doesn't even get planted; it's as if it were seed sitting on a rock. We all know those who have heard about God's Word and their hearts are so hard they reject it outright. (Hopefully we are not that way.) The second heart (the stony heart) has a moment of excitement, but that doesn't last long. As soon as the person hears a conflicting opinion, they begin to question the word. The third heart (the thorny heart) is probably the one committed Christians have to guard against. In the third case, the person receives the Word and begins to produce fruit, but doesn't stay focused. Either good things of the world get him distracted or the evil things get him in doubt and he abandons what he really knows.

As my husband and I have pastored our church, we have encountered many new believers. Often times they would begin their new life with great joy. They would encourage us as they shared special words from the Lord. They were filled with expectation about God working in their lives. Then, in some cases, circumstances - good or bad- would distract them from their walk.

One fine young man, Gene, came to the Lord and received deliverance from alcohol. He was thrilled and so appreciative of his Lord. After a few years, he wanted to make a career change, and so we prayed for a new job. That came also, but what followed was disappointing. Now with his new life and new career, Gene stopped spending as much time in the Word and missed church more often. We could see the thrill leave him as he pursued his new venture. Sadly, the day came when he walked away completely. It's as if he forgot all that the Lord had done for him. He tried to pretend that he was still spending time with the Lord, but it was easy to see that he was only pretending. Eventually the old problems were troubling him again.

In Jane's case, a difficult situation is what drew her away. She also received Jesus and began her new life with Him. Jane was one of the most ardent workers we have ever had, helping the church in any way she could. Jane studied the Word and shared with all those around her. She was truly an inspiration. However, her marriage hit some hard spots and she became very discouraged. We tried to help her see that the answers were with the Lord and His Word, but she just couldn't see. She was too busy trying to fix her problem with natural things. Eventually Jane also stopped her walk with the Lord.

It's easy to see that good things or unfortunate things can pull us away from our focus on God's Word. But the great treasure is for those who continue their divine pursuit. When we study the Bible, we must realize we are doing it for our own good. We are the ones who benefit by our study; we are not doing it out of obligation. As we study, we grow in our ability to appropriate all that God has for us.

The fourth heart is the one we want to have. It's the heart that hears God's Word and receives it. If we have this heart, we are teachable. When we see something in the Word for the first time, we are ready to hear and ready to do what He says. Furthermore, the fourth heart holds onto the Word and refuses to let it go.

Let me give you an example. Earlier I mentioned a couple who came to the Lord in mid-life. They had two sons who were on drugs and financing their habits by robbing stores. My friends saw in the Word a special promise from God. He said, "All of your children will be taught of the Lord. And the well-being of your sons will be great." (Isaiah 54:13) Clearly, at that time, the sons were not listening to their parents as they tried to bring counsel, and it was obvious that this Word didn't look like it was true in their situation. They could have easily given up - and many parents would have. But this couple refused to let go of the Word. They held on to it and reminded themselves daily about their promise from God. Eventually, they saw the Word fulfilled.

The Word is food for our spirits. We would never stop eating natural food. We would die. In the same way, we must continue with the nourishment of God's Word. If we will allow ourselves to do that, we will bear much fruit.

The first fruit we produce is faith. If we "hold on" to what we read in God's Word we will find ourselves growing in our faith - we will believe God more. When we read something, it will speak to us - we will hear God more. As we see the wonderful moments in the scripture we will begin to see ourselves there also. We will know our God better – His nature and His miraculous power.

Only when the Word of God is planted in your heart, can it produce for you

---

Often when I am teaching, I will take large seeds, such as acorns, to the session. I give one to each person and ask her to meditate on what she is holding. Within each seed is God's programming to produce. Each seed will produce after its kind – and only after its kind. Corn seeds produce corn; tomato seeds produce tomatoes. Also, you may notice that although the ability to produce is within the seed, it will only produce when it is planted. The outer shell has to disintegrate and the seed has to put down roots in the soil before a plant is produced. The seed has to be planted in good soil.

God's Word is the same. If you take twenty Bibles, scatter them around your house, and never open them, they will have no impact on your life. They may look pretty. They may even impress your friends. But they will not change your life. Only when the Word is planted in your heart – by reading it, or having it spoken to you, can it produce for you.

When the Word is planted in your honest and good heart, it will produce! We don't have to "make" it produce. It produces by itself.

Mark 4:26-29

And He was saying, "The kingdom of God is like a man who casts seed upon the soil; and goes to bed at night and gets up by day, and the seed sprouts up and grows – how he himself does not know. The soil produces crops by itself; first the blade, then the head, then the mature grain in the head."

How do we "plant" the seed? We spend time with our Father and His Word everyday. Sometimes we will be reading certain chapters through, and we will just pick up where we left off. On other occasions, we will need a certain word for the moment. Very often I will sit down with His Word in my lap. I will begin to praise Him and worship Him. Then I will just ask Him, "What do You want to say to me?" Or if I am facing a special crisis, I will say, "I need for You to give me direction."

Just like oil from Heaven, His presence seems to pour over me, and I know some answers. He may point me to a particular Word. He may speak something to me directly and then confirm it in His Word. He may remind me of a Word I know already. The main thing is my Father wants to communicate with me through His Word and He will do it again and again.

As a result of our choice to spend that time with our Father and His Word, we will find our faith and wisdom growing. First the blade, then the head, then the mature grain in the head. We will get answers – understanding – wisdom beyond our natural ability. All wisdom, knowledge, and empowerment

---

Just like oil from Heaven, His presence seems to pour over me

---

are wrapped up in God's Word. He has such a desire to give it to us.

Another way we plant the Word is to meditate upon it. The word "meditate" literally means "to mutter or murmur." That is eye-opening, isn't it? As we think about the Word and speak it to ourselves (some people call this "confessing the Word") we are planting the seed in our hearts. It grows by itself. The more we say it, the more we believe it. As a result of our meditating on the Word, faith is produced in our hearts.

You have an adventure awaiting you. Your Creator wants to share some secrets with you personally. He is waiting.

Revelation 3:20
Behold, I stand at the door and knock; if anyone hears
My voice and opens the door, I will come in to him, and
I will dine with him, and he with Me.

I urge you now to open the door. Talk to Him. Listen to Him. Let Him reveal His Word to you. All of God's truth is in His Word and He wants to reveal it to you. This miraculous Book is your most important possession. Your adventure is just beginning!

Let's Go Deeper

1. Read Matthew 13:3-23 and Luke 8:4-15

"The Sower Sows the Word" in two other accounts. What does Luke's account add that gives you more clarity about the process?

2. Write down some times when you have been tempted away from the Word because of affliction or persecution. What are some cares or desires which try to draw you away from God and His Word? Be honest with yourself. You don't have to tell anyone but your Father.

As the deer
pants for
the water brooks,
so my soul
pants for Thee,
O God
Psalm 42:1

Chapter Five
We Need Water

As Jesus taught, He used many different examples to get His truth across. The Master often told stories which helped His disciples to understand important things about the kingdom. We've talked about how Jesus compared God's Word to seed. Throughout the Bible, the Holy Spirit also compared God's Word to water.

To gain a different perspective, let's see how the Bible compares God's Word to water.

Isaiah 55:10-11
For as the rain and snow come down from heaven,
And do not return there without watering the earth,
And making it bear and sprout,
And furnishing seed to the sower and bread to the eater;
So shall My Word be which goes forth from My mouth,
It shall not return to Me empty,
Without accomplishing what I desire,
And without succeeding in the matter for which I sent it.

We'll talk more about this passage later. For now, let's just see that God's Word is referred to as water or snow.

I Corinthians 3: 6

I planted, Apollos watered, but God was causing the growth

How did they plant and water? They each spoke the Word. They planted God's truth. Paul calls it "seed" and "water."

In Ephesians, husbands are told to treat their wives as Jesus treated the church.

Ephesians 5:25-27

Husbands, love your wives, just as Christ
also loved the church and gave Himself for her;
that He might sanctify her,
having cleansed her by the washing of water
with the Word,
That He might present to Himself the church
in all her glory, having no spot or wrinkle
or any such thing,
but that she should be holy and blameless.

Jesus washes or cleanses us with the water of the Word. Again, the Word is water.

In all these verses, the Holy Spirit is comparing the Word to water. But how are they alike? We can see now how the Word is like seed. But how is it like water? Just as the seed is important to plant in your heart, so the water is necessary to water it. We are farmers of God's Word. Our farm land is our hearts. We have to plant the seed and then we have to water it – more meditation. More speaking the Word. More faith!

So what is so special about water that makes the Holy Spirit want to make that comparison? When we look at the next scripture, we should see it!

Psalm 147:15-20

He sends forth His command to the earth

His Word runs very swiftly.

He gives snow like wool;

He scatters the frost like ashes.

He casts forth His ice as fragments;

Who can stand before His cold?

He sends forth His Word and melts them

He causes the wind to blow and the waters to flow.

He declares His Words to Jacob

His statutes and His ordinances to Israel.

He has not dealt thus with any nation;

And as for His ordinances, they have not known them.

Can you see what He is saying? This is so clear, isn't it? God is comparing His Word to water and snow. But, hang on, here comes a great principle: the first speaking is referred to as "snow." It's too cold. No one can stand before it. Then there is a second speaking, and the water melts and flows and brings insight to the sons of Jacob. (That's us!)

The first speaking is the Bible which our Father sent to the earth: His miraculous speaking. But it is frozen, locked up so that we might not understand it. But then the second speaking is when the Holy Spirit REVEALS the written Word to our hearts. Suddenly the snow melts and the waters begin to flow. We understand it. Our precious friend, the Holy Spirit reveals God's Word and it becomes a part of us. We know secrets we never knew before. We understand mysteries which were heretofore unavailable.

I see the "seed principle" and the "water principle" as two ways of saying something similar. Just as the seed can't produce until it is planted and germinates in your heart, neither can the water become active in your life while it is still in "snow" form. Only the melted snow flows and soaks into the soil of your heart, bringing God's Word into your life.

Just as I have brought seeds to my teachings, I have on occasion brought ice cubes in a glass. As I teach, the ice cubes begin to melt. I hold up the glass and show two forms of water. You can't put ice cubes around your house plants and expect your desired results. The ice must melt to water the plant.

So what exactly am I saying? The snow is the Word spoken first – the Bible. People can have Bibles in their possession and yet never benefit from them. It's not just the existence of the Word that affects your life. The Word must speak to you. It can't be locked up as ice; it must flow like water. This comes by spending time with God and His Word. He will begin to take the words off the pages of your Bible and melt them. As He does, they will speak to you.

There are two Greek words for "word." One is "Logos," and it means the Word of the Bible. The second is "Rhema." That is when God speaks to you, or the Word is revealed to you. You will be reading a verse you have read many times, and suddenly it will seem to leap off the page. You will "see" something you never saw before. That is Rhema. That is God revealing His Word to you.

Effective prayer is based on Rhema- God's Word revealed to you personally. Your sister may eat good healthy food but what she eats won't help you. She may share with you her nutrition articles and delicious recipes, but you still will not benefit personally. Only when YOU eat the proper food will the benefit come to you.

God's Word works the same way. Your sister may have

a powerful walk with the Lord- based on His Word. She may share scriptures with you often. She even may try to make you see what she sees. But it doesn't happen that way. Only the Word which you allow God to speak to you personally will bring the nourishment of faith and wisdom to you.

Romans 10:17 says it best:
Now faith comes by hearing,
and hearing by the Word of God.

Faith doesn't just come by the Word, it comes by hearing the Word. The Greek word for "hearing" is rhema. So faith comes by the rhema which comes from spending time in the Word. Faith comes when the frozen Word is melted and revealed to you by the Holy Spirit.

When Jesus walked the earth, His persecution came from the religious leaders of the day. The Pharisees and Saducees were students of the scripture and knew what it said. Yet because of their hard hearts, they didn't understand the Word. They didn't even recognize the Messiah when He came. (Mark 4:12)

In my own life, I spent many years studying the Bible without recognizing it as God's Word. I had no revelation of the miracles which were available to me. But when I received Jesus and began my walk with Him, my eyes were opened. I began to see what the Word really said and I began to believe it. No longer was I depressed and overwhelmed. I knew that My Lord was working on behalf of my children and I knew that I could trust His love for them. Rhema came and so did faith!

When I committed my life to Jesus and began to walk with Him, my eyes were opened. I began to see what the Word really said, and I began to believe it.

As He taught, Jesus said, "He who has ears to hear, let him hear."(Mark 4:8) Everyone standing there must have had ears. He was speaking of spiritual ears, or the ability to receive the rhema from God. That's what we want! We want to have the ability not only to hear the Word with our natural ears, but with our spiritual ears as well. We want to hear God speak and His Word revealed.

In summary, when we spend time with God and His Word our faith level rises and we come up higher. When we read or hear the Word, we increase our ability to really hear: to have God's rhema come our way. Everything changes – for the better. We enter into a new level of understanding and power. We begin to walk with Him in His realm and operate in His principles.

Let's Go Deeper

Read Mark 4:24-25

1. Do you have an "ear to hear?"

2. Think of some times when you have honored God's Word and then received more.

3. Write down some thoughts about how you would like to increase your hearing and understanding.

Section Two

*...and he led me
through the
water,
water up
to the knees*

*Praise the Lord
in song,
for He has done
excellent things.
Let this be known
throughout the earth
Isaiah 12:5*

Chapter Six
The Big Picture

While in the second grade, my grandaughter Lauren was required to give a report on the state of her choice. (Needless to say, we were delighted when our Atlanta-born grandchild chose our state, Mississippi). Her accompanying prop was a poster with information about the state. Right in the center of her poster was a tiny dot and the words "Blue Mountain" (our town). She had cut the dot and words from a map of Mississippi. As I saw the tiny dot and words out of context, I couldn't help but smile.

This is the way many of us approach God's Word. We pick out verses we like and put them on our refrigerators. Very often, the context is ignored and the meaning lost. Context is essential if we are to understand what God means.

I prefer what I call the "satellite approach." Have you seen a spy movie in which surveillance techniques were used? While looking for someone in, say, Africa, the satellite camera will first observe the entire continent. Then the satellite will zoom to the area and the country. Finally the spies will find their subjects in a small tent in a remote part of the desert.

That's the way we should be with the Bible. We should get the big picture first – and then all the pieces on which we focus will be more meaningful.

So what is the big picture? The big picture has to have Jesus at the center. Why did Jesus come to earth? Why did He die on the cross? Let's look at the big picture.

Our scan should start at the beginning. If you look back at Genesis, it's clear that God created a perfect world and put His man and woman at its center.

Genesis 1:27,28

And God created man in His own image, in the image of God He created him; male and female He created them.

And God blessed them and said to them, "Be fruitful and multiply, and fill the earth, and subdue it; and rule over the fish of the sea and over the birds of the sky, and over every living thing that moves on the earth."

This man was given dominion over all things on the earth. So what is "dominion?" It is the assignment to rule the earth. He was to "subdue the earth and rule over it." God was the CEO, but Adam was to be God's manager of the earth.

There was only one catch. This man could run the earth as long as he represented God, his Creator. If Adam let the devil influence him, he would lose his place. He couldn't rule over Satan and be ruled by him at the same time.

As we continue to read in Genesis, we see that the devil tempted Eve and she disobeyed God. Then Adam followed suit, and the two got fired as God's managers. Adam and Eve bowed to the devil and lost their place. God would not allow His power to be used by the devil. Adam and Eve lost their position, and they lost their ability to communicate with God. Their spirits became separated from their Creator.

From the time of the fall,
God was looking for a man
who would truly believe Him
and be faithful to Him

From the time of the fall, God was looking for a man who would truly believe Him and be faithful to Him. He was planning to nurture that man and his heirs and teach them His ways. Then eventually He would bring through that family His own Son, conceived by His Holy Spirit. God found that man in Abraham, made a covenant with him, and began developing his family – the nation of Israel.

During that time, a little more than 1400 years, the devil ran rampant throughout the earth. Only the nation of

---

A new breed was created - men and women in covenant with God

Israel was being led and guided by God. That's why they were called "His chosen people." They were the only group of people in covenant with God. They were learning who He was – His character and His ways.

After many centuries of this covenant relationship with this one group of people, God brought forth His Son, the second Adam, Jesus. He walked the earth for about 33 years, showing those around Him how God's man should live. He went to the cross, taking the penalty for man's sinful nature, descended into Hell, reclaimed dominion, and on the third day arose from the dead. He then ascended into Heaven to be seated on the right hand of His Father and sent His Holy Spirit back to earth. The Holy Spirit came back to live in the hearts of those who believe Him and commit to Him.

Thus a new covenant was cut by His precious blood, and a new breed was created on earth – men and women cleansed by His blood, filled with the Holy Spirit, and in covenant with their God. With the Holy Spirit living in them, they could once again communicate with their Creator. They could hear His voice, understand His Word, and live on the earth as God had intended.

Remember I mentioned earlier the "rules of the universe" which our Father set up in the beginning? As I said earlier, one of those rules was that God had wanted His man to rule with Him. He had wanted Adam to represent Him and to rule according to His plan and purpose. Adam was supposed to dress and "keep" the garden, kicking out the devil instead of listening to him. God had wanted for there to be a joint effort between Himself and His man.

What Adam wouldn't do, Jesus did - and more! Jesus restored the authority to rule. Mankind had the opportunity to be restored back to the place of Adam!

I say "opportunity" because this covenant was for those who believed and received Jesus as their Lord. This new covenant was not for just anyone, but for those who accepted the blood sacrifice of Jesus for themselves. This new covenant was offered to the Jews and to those who weren't Jews. It was offered to all people. Those who received that blood sacrifice and partook of the covenant entered into a wonderful relationship with God. To those people God began restoring dominion. Such a plan! Such a privilege!

Let's talk a little more about the word "dominion." The Hebrew word is "radah," which means "to rule, to reign, to tread down, or to cause to crumble." So Adam was indeed given the commission to rule and reign over the earth, as long as he represented God. He lost that ability through disobedience. Then Jesus returned it to us.

In Matthew 28:18 Jesus said, "All authority has been given unto Me. Go, therefore…" This word, "authority" is the Greek word "exousia" which has a meaning similar to the Hebrew word for "dominion." So Jesus is saying that the dominion given to Adam has been restored to Him. He doesn't say that it's restored to everyone, but to Jesus. Therefore when He says, "go," He is talking to those who go in His name. Though this authority is offered to everyone, the prerequisite for accepting it is to represent Jesus and His Kingdom. Only those who represent Him and His Father have that authority or dominion restored.

So here we stand today. We are born of God and filled with His Spirit. We have the right to rule over the sphere our

Father has given us. NEVER DO WE RULE OVER OTHER PEOPLE. Even though we have a certain "rule" over our children when they are children, when they are grown, we no longer have that rule. God has given every man free will. Even He will not violate that will, therefore, neither can we nor should we try. The devil tries to dominate man. If we were to try to dominate others, we would be operating in the devil's manner.

So what do we rule? We rule over demons and natural forces. We may even commission angels. Our restored ability is to push back the forces of darkness which blind and hinder others. Those evil forces can keep our loved ones in confusion and rebellion against God. But as we rule over those forces, that darkness must flee from them. This is a huge part of our ability in prayer: our authority to push back the forces of darkness.

Where do we rule? We rule within the sphere our Father has given us. II Corinthians 10:13 calls it a "measure of rule" apportioned to us by God. We might say that our "measure of rule" (or "sphere") is where we have been assigned by God. Obviously our homes will be our first sphere, then our ministries, our places of work, and then the geographical area where God has placed us.

We have great authority over demons in places where God has placed us, but not in other places. My husband and I have ruling authority in our home, but not in yours. I have no authority in your home, unless you ask me to pray, but even then the authority is limited. Your home is your assignment from God.

The same applies to ministries, churches, businesses, or governments. Successful ruling comes by being commissioned there by God. Occasionally you will hear of outsiders coming into churches and trying to take over services, saying they are sent by God. They are mistaken. Those people have stepped out of their sphere and are not operating with Godly authority.

How do we rule? We must represent God and His desires. When we come under the influence of the devil or our flesh, we lose our position – just as Adam did. In the first chapter of Genesis, the Holy Spirit speaks of the sun ruling the day and the moon ruling the night. Jesus is like the sun; we are like the moon. He is a source of light; we are only a reflection of His light. When the earth stands between the sun and the moon, only a partial moon appears – sometimes a complete eclipse. In the same way, when our flesh stands between Jesus and ourselves, we are only partial reflections. Our goal is to represent, or reflect, Jesus in such completeness we will be like full moons. The more we reflect Him, the more we influence the darkness around us.

Our authority is given when we represent Jesus. We

have to rule in accordance with His plans and we have to represent the love of God.

My husband has a great analogy. Ephesians 3:17 says we are to be "rooted and grounded in love." He says that love is the grounding wire in our lives just as an electrical outlet has a grounding wire. When the grounding wire is not connected, the circuit is disabled and the power doesn't flow. When we are not grounded in love, it's as if we have flipped the circuit breaker and His power is turned off.

That concept is so true. Our Father will not allow His power to be used for evil! When we have selfish, evil motives, we lose our ability to take dominion – even within our designated sphere.

We want to be full moons, reflecting Jesus in completeness

So let's summarize. Through the death, burial, and resurrection of Jesus and our commitment to Him, we have a privilege and responsibility restored to us. We have the right to take dominion, or rule, in our own sphere. Yet we have to do this within the boundaries our Father has given to us. We must also keep the position by being obedient to our Father and operating in love.

If you have never heard any teaching about this authority, you may find yourself being stretched at this point. I pray that you will be like the men of Berea. (Acts 17:11). Paul had been preaching to the Jews in other places that the Messiah had come. Only a few had received the truth. The men of Berea were more honorable. They searched the scriptures to see if Paul's preaching was true, and they found that it was so. If you search the scriptures, you will see these things to be so.

Take some time at this point. Pray for the Father to show you what He wants you to know. Be willing to learn something new from your Father and His Word. He wants to take you into deeper water. As you continue reading, things will come into greater focus.

Let's Go Deeper

1 Read II Corinthians 10:13

Write a few words about your "measure of rule."
Where has God called you? Where do you have
the authority to rule the atmosphere?

2. Read Acts 17:11

Do you consider yourself like the "men of Berea?"
In what way?

Do not fear,
Abram,
I am a shield to you.
Your reward
will be
very great.
Genesis 15:1

Chapter Seven

Abraham,
Who Are You?

N ow that we have the big picture, let's get our zoom lens working. Let's zoom in on some bits and pieces of what we have talked about. The zoom will help us to see things better.

In the next chapter we are going to discuss the blessings of Abraham, but before we do that, we need to take a good look at Abraham. Who was he? What was so special about him that God would choose him? Let's look closely.

Genesis 12-22 tell us all about it. We will summarize in this way: When God called Abraham, his name was Abram, Hebrew for "High Father." God called him out of his land and away from his family. (Back in those days, travel was hard. When you left your family and went into another land, you probably would never see them again). This was a very difficult decision to make, but he obeyed God. God promised that if he would leave, he would be blessed, and through him all the nations of the earth would be blessed. (Of course, He was speaking of Jesus). Hebrews 11:8 says that he didn't know where he was going, but he followed God's call because he believed in Him and trusted Him. He and his wife, Sarai, Hebrew for "Contentious One," along with his nephew, Lot, went to Canaan and lived in tents. They couldn't settle there, because the time wasn't right. There was even famine in the land from time to time, but they lived there because God had called them to do it.

As time went on, God did bless Abram and he became very rich. The Word says that after several years, he and Lot had so much livestock that their herdsmen argued about the grazing land. There wasn't enough room for all of their animals. So Abram suggested that they move away from each other. He allowed Lot to choose first the land he wanted, then Abram took the other. You can see that Abram was a giver, can't you?

However, even though Abram was rich, what he really wanted was an heir. Abram and Sarai had no children and he considered the greatest treasure would be a son. Over the years Abram had several encounters with God in which God made promises of blessings. Yet Abram still had no son.

In Genesis chapter 15, God appeared to Abram and established a covenant with him. As Abram brought the required sacrifices, he fell into a deep sleep and God spoke to him. Speaking of Abram's heirs who would eventually possess Canaan, God unfolded the future. Abram's descendants were to go into a land that was not theirs. They would stay there for 400 years and serve the strangers. At the end of that time, they would come out with "great possessions" and enter into the land of Canaan. (Indeed all of this did eventually come true, as Abram's descendants went into Egypt).

There was just one problem with God's prophecy: Abram had no children. He was already an old man, and he and Sarai had a hard time seeing how God was going to do what He said. (Have you ever been there? Sometimes what God promises seems impossible. But with God all things are possible).

So Abram and Sarai took a detour and decided they needed to help God out. Sarai suggested that Abram conceive with her maid. He did, and Ishmael was born, but quickly it was obvious that God's blessing was not there. As you can imagine, strife broke out between Sarai and her maid, Hagar.

Time went by. Then when Abram was 99 years old, God appeared to him and spoke again. He reiterated His plan to bless all the earth through the seed of Abram. This time He stepped it up. He told Abram that He was changing his name to Abraham, which means "the Father of Many Nations." He also changed Sarai's name to Sarah, "Princess." God directed Abraham to circumcise himself and all his household. In the future, He wanted all males born as descendants to be circumcised on the eighth day. That circumcision was a sign of the covenant between Abraham and his heirs and God Almighty. God also told Abraham that the child of promise was to come through his wife, Sarah.

Now let's remember that Abraham was not born again. He didn't have the Holy Spirit within him teaching him. He was a natural man who had an awe-inspiring ability to believe God and trust Him. God was planning to raise up a group of people who would be the ones to bring the Messiah, the Savior, to the world. He needed to find someone who believed Him and someone who would be willing to give his all to the Lord. Then God would give His all to that man. That special person would be God's covenant partner in His plan for salvation.

Abraham proved himself to be that man. Even though he was 99 years old, Romans 4:19, 20 says that

> *"And without becoming weak in faith, he contemplated his own body, now as good as dead, since he was about a hundred years old, and the deadness of Sarah's womb; yet with respect to the promise of God, he did not waver in unbelief, but grew strong in faith, giving glory to*

*God. and being fully assured that what He had prom-
ised, He was also able to perform.*

Wow! I have to admit that I know very few people who
believe God the way Abraham did. How about you? Do you
think that you could believe extreme promises which your Father might make to you? Well, your Father HAS made extreme
promises to you. In the next chapter we will look at some of
these extreme promises.

Abraham was a natural man with an awe-inspiring ability to believe God and to trust Him

---

Right now, let's pull back another curtain on the life of
Abraham. The promise was fulfilled and Sarah gave birth to
Isaac. After his son, Isaac, was a young boy and the promise
seemed complete, God made a strange request. He said for
Abraham to take Isaac up on the mountain and sacrifice him.
This is indeed a strange request and one which has been misin-
terpreted many times. We know that God would never expect
us to sacrifice our children – such an idea would be abhorrent
to Him. Abraham knew that also. Therefore, he was obedient
to take his son and firewood up the mountain, saying that they
were going to "worship." Isaac asked his father where the sac-

rificial lamb was. Abraham said, "God will provide the lamb." As we read in Genesis we see that Abraham bound his son to the altar and had a knife in his hand raised for slaughter before the angel told him to stop and a ram was waiting in the bushes. The Lord had indeed "provided a lamb."

There is a great mystery involved when we make a covenant with the Creator of the Universe. He created us, yet He wants to be in covenant with us. Isn't that amazing? He wants to make an agreement – a sort of contract – which will benefit both of us. This is the really amazing part: He let's US decide how big the partnership will be.

God's kingdom principle of sowing and reaping is a major teaching throughout the gospels.

Luke6:38

Give and it shall be given to you, good measure, pressed down, shaken together, running over, they will pour into your lap. For by your standard of measure it will be measured to you in return.

Your "standard of measure" will decide your walk with the Lord. Because of your free will, YOU get to decide how much of God's involvement you have in your life. Do you want a small amount of His involvement in your life? That's easy. Just give Him a small amount of yourself. Do you want all your Father has to offer? Give Him everything you have.

When God called Abraham to sacrifice Isaac, He had no intention of there being a human sacrifice. Of course He didn't! But He allowed Abraham the opportunity to show his faith and commitment. He gave his all to God, and that paved the way for God to give His all to Abraham. This act of obedience made it so that God could offer His Son, Jesus, as a sacrifice through Abraham's lineage. It comprised the most complete covenant imaginable.

God created us, yet He wants us to be in covenant with Him

I believe that the bottom line is this: God was looking for a specific person who could be the father of the nation which would bring the Savior. He had to be a man of total commitment. As Abraham proved himself, he became that man.

In this day, the Savior has come, but He is still looking for people who will commit to fulfill His plan. He is looking for those who say, "Not my will, but Thine, Oh Lord." He is not asking us to offer up physical sacrifices. He wants us to offer ourselves as "living sacrifices."(Romans 12:1). He desires people who want God's will in their lives, knowing they can trust His plan and His goodness. These people want to live their lives according to His purpose, knowing that as they do, they will be able to help others to know their Father and His precious Son. The people who are willing to walk in that realm of faith and commitment make themselves available to see the miraculous hand of God in their own lives.

He is still looking for people who will commit to fulfill His plan

---

So how committed are you? Do you truly want God's will in your life? Are you like Abraham and know that His will is only good and perfect? Do you understand that your Heavenly Father loves you more than you can imagine? Do you understand that He can and will do far more than you can ask or think when your heart is toward Him? (Ephesians 3:20)

One way we can test ourselves in this area is to ask the question, "What do I do when I am alone? Do I have a heart that praises Him? Am I as dedicated to Him when no one is watching as I am when others are around?" Human nature makes us want to look good to others. We will show our best face in church or around other Christians. The big question is, "What do we do when no one is watching?" That's who we really are!

In the pages ahead we will touch on several different

aspects of your faith-life. Your commitment, His promises, His plan of prayer. All of these topics are designed to lead you closer to a true understanding of your role as a praying mom. Hopefully, as we progress you will begin to see yourself differently. You will see yourself as a chosen one, a loved one, a victorious child of God. And you will begin to see His promises of good for your children. His plan is great. His plan is perfect. It's up to us to get in on it!

Let's Go Deeper

1. Read Genesis, chapters 12-22

   Write about what you have learned. Do you see

   yourself in those pages? Explain.

2. Read Romans 4:13-25

   Write about your insights.

3. Read Hebrews 11:8-12

   In what way do you want to be like Abraham?

*And I
will establish
My covenant
between
Me and you
Genesis 17:2*

Chapter Eight

Blessings
Of Abraham

As mothers, we know how much we love our children and how much we are always pulling for them. In the same way, God is always pulling for us. Isn't that comforting? The love we have for our children doesn't even compare to His love for us – and our children. That boggles the mind, but it's true.

Now let's return to Abraham's story: God found a man who really wanted children – and one who would believe Him. Then He gave him a son, Isaac, and many descendants who eventually made up the nation of Israel. They were His covenant people. Just as God had spoken to Abraham, his descendants went into Egypt and served another people. Then He brought them out by a mighty hand – with many signs and wonders- and settled them in the land of Canaan.

For nearly two thousand years there was only one group of people with whom our Father had a covenant. Does that mean that He didn't love the others? No. He did love all men. He had no desire for the world to be in the shape it was. However, He honored the free will He had given men and after the fall of Adam, the devil seemed to rule.

So God developed a relationship with one group of people. This one group came about when God was looking for a man WHO WOULD BELIEVE HIM, and He found Abraham. Not only did Abraham believe Him, but the Word says that God knew that Abraham would teach his children about Him. Most men were not able to understand God or to communicate with Him very well. He wanted to nurture a family of people who could receive from Him, obey Him, and be a representation to the world about the goodness of God. More importantly, He wanted to find a family who could receive and raise a Savior according to God's plan.

Our Creator chose Abraham because he believed and obeyed God when He spoke to him. Our Father also knew that he would teach his children about his God. So the Creator of the Universe made a covenant with Abraham – a contract. As we saw in the chapters of Genesis, their covenant was that Abraham would walk with God and be obedient to Him. God, in turn, would bless Abraham abundantly. He would be his defender, his provider, his healer, his all-in-all. He promised him a miracle son and promised also that someday his heirs would possess Canaan, the Promised Land.

As Abraham's family grew, their covenant with God became more and more defined. After several hundred years, when Abraham's descendants were in slavery in Egypt, God was ready to show the world this covenant which had been contracted hundreds of years before. With a mighty hand and many signs and wonders, the God of Abraham (That's how He identified Himself – what a covenant-keeper!) delivered the nation of Israel from the Pharaoh's evil iron fist. He led the millions of people out of Egypt, parted the Red Sea so that they could go across, and eventually led them into the Promised Land of Canaan.

Their unbelief kept them from going into the Promised Land

If you know the Bible, you know that these Israelites who left Egypt messed up in the desert. After all the miracles they had seen, they got scared and didn't believe that God could give them the Promised Land. Their unbelief kept them from going into the Land. Instead that particular generation had to wander in the wilderness for 40 years.

God's will was to take them into Canaan immediately, but they nullified that part of their covenant when they wouldn't believe God's Word. Hebrews 4:2 explains it: the promise made to them "didn't profit them, because the promise was not mixed with their faith!" But God didn't relinquish His promise to Abraham. Even though this generation disqualified themselves, He waited for the next generation. Then when He could find people who believed Him, He took them into the Land He had promised.

During the time in the wilderness, Moses was the leader. He had several visitations from God, bringing laws and principles which would guide the lives of these special people. He also gave them ordinances concerning religious feasts and sacrifices which would foreshadow God's sacrifice of His own

---

Believing in God, His goodness, and His Word is always essential to receiving His blessings

---

Son. All of the laws and ordinances were to show them who He was, and to lead them to the eventual understanding of His Son, Jesus, the Messiah. This family, this nation, was still in covenant with their God.

In Deuteronomy 28, Moses shared the most detailed word about the "Blessings of Abraham." As the people stood and listened, their leader, Moses, shared the word that God had given him. He carefully listed the blessings they could expect if they were obedient to God. He also listed the curses which would come upon them if they were disobedient. This scripture is so significant. First it shows God's will for those who are in covenant with Him. The curses are never His will for His covenant people. But just as the earlier generation couldn't enter the Promised Land because of their unbelief, neither could these people receive these blessings without faith. Believing in God, His goodness, and His Word is always essential to receiving the blessings He has to extend.

Now this is where we come in. Let's take a look at our scripture promise: Galatians 3:13,14

> *Christ redeemed us from the curse of the law, having become a curse for us-for as it is written, "Cursed is everyone who hangs on a tree"*
> *In order that in Christ Jesus the blessing of Abraham might come to the gentiles, so that we might receive the promise of the Spirit through faith.*

This says that Jesus became a curse for us that we might receive the Blessing of Abraham. This is huge! We have been grafted into the original covenant – and we have a better covenant. These blessings are for us.

If you want to know what God's will is for you, meditate on Deuteronomy 28. His will is for your obedience to Him and His will is for the blessings to be manifested in your life.

In Acts 1:8 Jesus tells the disciples that when the Holy Spirit comes upon them they will have power to "be His witnesses." It doesn't just say "to witness," but to "be a witness." I think that one way we "are witnesses," is that our lives testify of God's goodness. People see us blessed and glorify God because of it. I'm not saying we have a problem-free life. I am saying that when we have problems, we overcome. An overcoming life is one that goes through the problems which may come and presses through to the other side where blessings abound.

One way we are witnesses is that our lives testify of God's goodness

---

Many Christians call these promises listed in Deuteronomy 28 our "Promised Land." Faith is required to enter this Land. Just as the children of Israel missed their blessing because of unbelief, many Christians miss receiving these promises because of unbelief. Indeed, many don't know about these promises. Some even discount anyone who talks about the blessings of God.

I don't want to be like that. Do you? I want to understand and receive everything my Father has for me. I want to know about the promises, and I want to believe them. What Jesus has done for us is greater than anyone can imagine! Only by spending time with our Father can we begin to see the greatness of our covenant.

Psalm 116 says,
How can I repay Him for all His goodness toward me?
I will lift up my cup and drink from it and call upon
the name of the Lord.

That's the life I want. I want to live in communication with my Father and I want to believe Him in every promise He has made to me. I want to drink from the cup He has provided.

So what does our covenant entail? Deuteronomy 28 says it best. Remember this was spoken by Moses to the Israelites and Galatians 3:13,14 says this is for us also.

Deuteronomy 28:1-14
Now it shall be, if you will diligently obey the Lord
your God, being careful to do all His commandments

which I command you today, the Lord your God will set you high above all the nations of the earth.

And all these blessings shall come upon you and over-take you, if you will obey the Lord your God.

Blessed shall you be in the city, and blessed shall you be in the country.

Blessed shall be the offspring of your body and the produce of your ground and the offspring of your beasts, the increase of your herd and the young of your flock.

Blessed shall be your basket and your kneading bowl.

Blessed shall you be when you come in, and blessed shall you be when you go out.

The Lord shall cause your enemies who rise up against you to be defeated before you; they shall come out against you one way and shall flee before you seven ways.

The Lord will command the blessing upon you in your barns and in all that you put your hand to, and He will bless you in the land which the Lord your God gives you.

The Lord will establish you as a holy people to Himself, as He swore to you, if you will keep the commandments of the Lord your God, and walk in His ways.

So all the peoples of the earth shall see that you are called by the name of the Lord, and they shall be afraid of you.

And the Lord shall make you abound in prosperity, in the offspring of your body and in the offspring of your beast and in the produce of your ground, in the land which the Lord swore to your fathers to give you.

The Lord will open for you His good storehouse, the heavens, to give rain to your land in its season and to bless all the work of your hand; and you shall lend to many nations, but you shall not borrow.

And the Lord will make you the head and not the tail, and you only shall be above, and you shall not be underneath, if you will listen to the commandments of the Lord your God, which I charge you today, to observe them carefully,

And do not turn aside from any of the words which I command you today, to the right or the left, to go after other gods to serve them.

As you go through these verses, you will begin to find many of them which ring out to you as especially encouraging. In a nutshell, He promises provision, blessings on you and your family, and favor upon you. If you want to get an even clearer picture of God's will, continue in this chapter and read what He calls a curse. The curses include physical disease, lack of provision, and problems with your children. Those are never God's will for His covenant people. In this chapter we see so clearly that God wants good and not evil to come your way!

So let's get back to prayer — that is really what we are talking about, isn't it? If you notice in Deuteronomy 28, He promises that the "fruit of your womb" is blessed. Your children are blessed. Now at the moment, your children may not look very blessed. They may be walking away from God or they may be going through a tough time. That is where your faith is so important. You know your Father's will. He says it

---

Your children have their free will, but as you pray, all the forces of Heaven will work on your and their behalf

---

clearly: His will is for your children to be blessed. (This is based on YOUR covenant, not on theirs). Now your prayers of faith become like hands which reach out to receive what your Father has promised.

Your children have their free will, but as you pray, all

the forces of heaven will work on your and their behalf. As you stand on God's Word for your children, demons will have to flee. As you pray in agreement with God's will, angels will be assigned to bring them to the place of a right decision. They will have that chance again and again. Our God is faithful to His covenant. As you believe and do your part, you will see His Mighty hand demonstrate His goodness and His faithfulness.

I have heard many testimonies of God's faithfulness in fulfilling His covenant. Shannon and her husband were trying to walk with God to the best of their ability. Believing God was speaking to them, they moved their family across the country to a Bible school for ministry training. The children were enrolled in the Christian school on campus.

In the ministry school there were many people from across the country. They had come there because they had a desire to understand God and His Word better and to have a closer walk with Him. There was vibrant praise, lots of prayer, and lots of fellowship with the other believers. Shannon and her husband learned many truths while there, but there was one major problem. The leadership was legalistic, imposing harsh rules on the children, and Shannon's teenage daughter was hurt by such harshness.

Disappointed, the family left the school after one year, but the teenage daughter, Emily, was hurt and confused by her parents' decision to go to the school in the first place. The couple tried to help her recover, but the wound was deeper than they had thought and it took many years for recovery even to begin.

The parents continued to pray for God to intervene. As the daughter grew into adulthood, it seemed sometimes that she would not recover. The hurt was very deep. There was always a relationship with the parents, but this precious one found it very difficult to trust God. Prayers continued over the years.

Stand strong and you will see God's goodness

After many years, there was finally a breakthrough. A friend who had attended the same school, located Emily, who was now many miles away. They reestablished communication and for the first time, there seemed to come some healing. Never would Shannon have thought that this friend would be the one to minister to her daughter, but God knew. They shared hurts and disappointments. They became close friends again. The friendship was like a gold coin which Emily found in the mire of that experience. The last I heard, the healing wasn't complete, but it was well on its way. God is so faithful!

So you may have a child who has been hurt by religion. Maybe he was hurt because an authority figure he trusted fell into sin. Maybe she was hurt by legalism or harshness which didn't represent God. But don't give up! Keep praying for them. Keep believing God's blessing will be manifested upon that child. As you persist in prayer, He will bring just the right people into their lives- the ones who can help bring them healing and deliverance. Stand strong, and you will see God's goodness.

I have had many answers to prayer for my children because of knowing His will. When you know what God wants for you, you don't "give in" to evil that may come. You know to resist it as work from the devil. I will share one such experience.

When my son was about 18 months old, I took him to the doctor for a regular check up. He had no symptoms; it was just routine. I was shocked when the doctor said to me, "Your son has pneumonia. I'll give him a shot and some follow up medicine. Bring him back tomorrow, and if he's not better, I will hospitalize him."

After we had been home for a few hours, the symptoms burst forth! He spiked a very high fever, and developed lots of congestion. I was treating his fever with alcohol rubs and tepid water baths. We had a vaporizer running in his room. Of course, I was giving him the prescribed medicine – and praying. (I have to admit, my focus was on the medicine, not the prayer).

That night I slept on a cot in his room so I could listen out for his breathing. At about 4 o'clock in the morning, I had a dream. A very sweet voice said to me, "I am taking him home now. You have enjoyed him for awhile. Now I am taking him home so you will have more time for the ministry." If I had not known the Word, I may have thought that the voice was from the Lord. It sounded so sweet. But I knew my covenant. THAT WAS NOT THE LORD!!

I jumped out of bed and ran to get my husband. The two of us knelt by our son's bed and refused to get up until we saw him healed. After about an hour of intense prayer, his fever broke and we knew we had the victory. The next day when I took my son back to the doctor, HE was the one who was shocked. His remark: "I have never seen antibiotics work that fast!"

The point in this episode is that we must know God's will- God's covenant- or our prayers will be weak. Since we don't want to pray against God's will, if we don't know our covenant, we won't have the confidence necessary to see our prayers through to victory.

Our Father loves our children, and He wants them blessed. Let's reach out for that with everything in our beings. Let's commit to learning about and understanding just what our blessings are. And let's commit to appropriating all that our Father has for us.

Let's Go Deeper

1. Meditate on Deuteronomy 28

Write down some new understanding you may have about your covenant with God.

Are there some curses which bring you clarity about what your Father DOESN'T want for you?

*And a voice
out of heaven said,
"This is
My beloved Son,
in whom
I am well-pleased."
Matthew 3:17*

Chapter Nine

Jesus
Our Deliverer

We have been looking at the Abrahamic blessings and how Jesus brought them to us. Now we need to take a closer look at our new covenant.

When we accept Jesus as our Savior and Lord we come into a wonderful covenant with our Father. Instead of Abraham being our leader, or Moses being our leader, Jesus, the Son of God Himself, is now our leader. A miraculous life awaits us. You may study and study the Bible, but there will always be more to learn. And it's always better than you thought it would be! Paul prayed in Ephesians that they (and we) would know

> "the hope of His calling, the riches of the glory of His inheritance in the saints, and the exceeding greatness of His power toward those who believe." (Ephesians 1:18-19)

He also prayed that we "would be able to compre-

hend with all the saints what is the width and length
and depth and height – to know the love of God which
surpasses knowledge." (Ephesians 3: 18-19)

God's love surpasses knowledge. His plan surpasses knowledge. The magnitude of what Jesus has done for us surpasses knowledge. Let's look at the chapter in Isaiah which shows most clearly what our Savior has done. Now this is a covenant better than Abraham's!

Isaiah 53.4.
Surely, He has borne our griefs
and carried our sorrows
Yet we esteemed Him stricken,
smitten of God, and afflicted.
But He was wounded for our transgressions
He was bruised for our iniquities
The chastisement for our peace was upon Him.
And by His stripes we are healed.
All we like sheep have gone astray
We have turned, everyone, to his own way
And the Lord has laid on Him the iniquity of us all.

This chapter looks forward to the day the deliverer will come to Israel. Many of the Jews did not know that this deliverer would come for the world. They thought that their exclusive covenant would continue. But they knew that this Messiah would break off the chains of evil from their backs. They just didn't know how.

In the fullness of time, the Savior did come and pay that price. He "interceded for the transgressors."(Isaiah 53:12) So what does that mean? By His sacrifice, He stood as One who joined man back to God. It's as if He stood with one hand to Heaven and the other to earth. He was saying, "God, behold your man; he's clean now. Man, behold your God; He loves you."

It's as if Jesus stood with one hand to Heaven and the other to earth

---

This plan of salvation was really huge! Unfortunately, many people take bits and pieces of the plan. They know that Jesus died for our sins. They receive Him as their Savior, and they know that they will go to Heaven when they die. They even try to live good lives. But they don't understand the magnitude of God's salvation plan. They don't understand that Jesus restored us back to the place of Adam.

Others, more enlightened, have referred to this as the "great exchange." Man had sin, grief, anger, sickness, and torment. Jesus had none of these. He was a perfect man- with God's blood flowing through His veins. He had never sinned, had no sickness, no grief – just perfect peace. So He traded places with us.

He took our sin,
and gave us righteousness

Someone had to pay the price for all the imperfection in our lives. The Bible says that the "wages of sin is death." (Romans 6:23). There was a death penalty required for our sin, and Jesus paid that debt for us. He went to the cross and took the punishment we deserved. He went into hell and stayed there for three days. Then on the third day, He arose from the dead. A little later, after appearing to His disciples, He arose to Heaven to sit at the right hand of His Father.

On the cross He said, "It is finished." (John 19:30) The sacrifice was complete; He had paid the price for us. Until that time, the devil had been able to hold people captive at his will. The ransom for their deliverance was death to be paid by a perfect man. Jesus paid that price and handed us our ticket to liberty.

So He took our sin and gave us righteousness;

He took our grief and gave us peace;

He took our sorrows and gave us joy;

He took our sickness and gave us health.

This was indeed the greatest exchange the world had ever known. And now he says, "Behold I stand at the door and knock." We have to let Him in. We have to receive the gift. We have to believe in Him and allow Him to be our Lord.

The debt has been paid and we have been redeemed and restored. Now it's our option. Not everyone will partake of this redemption because they won't believe it. But it is available to BELIEVERS. Do you believe it? How much of it do you believe? You have to answer those questions for yourself. You also have to answer another question: how much of God do you really want in your life?

It's your choice. I pray that you choose wisely.

Choose life!

Let's Go Deeper

Read Isaiah 53

This chapter is the best account of the work
of the Messiah.

1. Write down your impressions about your Savior.

2. Pray that your Father will open up more truth to
you concerning this chapter.

Section Three

..and he led me through the water, water reaching the loins

*I am convinced
that God
does nothing
on earth
except in response
to believing prayer*

-John Wesley

Chapter Ten
Now Let's Pray

Let's keep moving. We are moving out into the water up to our loins. Now we are going to truly become "prayer warriors."

Have you ever wondered why we pray? Do you sometimes think that God wants us to beg Him for things? Do you think that He is indifferent to what is happening to you? Or that He doesn't know about your needs? Well, that's why we took so much time in laying our foundation. When we understand about the authority of God's Word, the importance of being born again, the covenant we have with Jesus, and our Father's love for us, it's so much easier to have God's plan come into focus.

First of all, put it to rest that your Father loves you. He only wants good for you. He doesn't get any pleasure from your begging Him, since He already wants the best for you.

So why do we pray? God gave man dominion on the

earth, and that has always been His plan. The reason you ask Him for things is because of your free will. He says to you, "What do you want?" God does not treat you as a puppet. He recognizes your individuality and your desires, even if they are wrong. He won't cross your will.

God's plan of prayer is really simple. Because of our free will, He wants us to ask Him for the things He has promised. Then He wants to bring these things to pass in the earth. He won't force His will upon us. He wants us to ask for it. He also wants us to use our dominion, our authority, to halt the devil's activity and to bring angels onto the scene.

Your heavenly Father comes to you when He is asked and He honors His Word in your life when you honor His Word: when you believe it and ask for it. Do you want to know His will? His will is His Word. It explains His covenant with us, and it shows how we appropriate it.

Remember, when you are a Christian, you are in covenant with God through Jesus. Read the Word to discover the details of your covenant: what God has promised you and what He expects from you. Then pray those promises back to God. You ask for His will to be done in your life. And you ask in specific terms.

Let's see it in the Bible.

I John 5:14,15

This is the confidence we have toward Him that if we ask anything according to His will, He hears us, and if He hears us, we know that we have the requests we have made of Him.

When you are praying for your children, there are many scriptures which show God's will for them. We have already talked about Deuteronomy 28. Let's look at some others.

Deuteronomy 30: 6

The Lord your God will circumcise your heart and the hearts of your descendants, to love the Lord your God with all your heart and with all your soul, in order that you may live.

Isaiah 54:13

And all your sons will be taught of the Lord; And the well-being of your sons will be great.

Psalm 112:1,2

How blessed is the man who fears the Lord Who greatly delights in His commandments His descendants will be mighty upon the earth.

I have read the Bible through, and I have never seen

anything that indicates that God ever wants to harm your children. Or that He is indifferent to their needs. From start to finish, it's clear that family is very important to God. He is the one who put that unconditional love in your heart for your children. He makes His will very apparent: He only wants the best for your offspring.

You may say that your son or daughter has gone too far. You may say that they have been involved in so much sin that there is no way back. I will say that there is nothing impossible for our God. When you know that it is ALWAYS God's will for your children to come to Him and to receive from Him, then your faith rises.

---

*It is always God's will
for your children to come to Him
and to receive from Him*

If you will work with God for His will to be done, it will be done. Your part is to pray and ask Him; His part is to accomplish it! You can't "make things happen." You cannot control your children. He won't control them, but He can get the job done. He knows just the right person to bring across their path to assist their progress. He can give them dreams.

He can cause the circumstances around them to change. Just trust Him and expect great things. When you are doing your part in prayer, your Heavenly Father is accomplishing the fulfillment you ask.

In Genesis 27-35, we see the story of Isaac's son, Jacob. He was to be the heir who would inherit Abraham's covenant, but Jacob had some problems. He tricked his father and stole the blessing which was intended for his brother, Esau. Then, fearing Esau's wrath, Jacob fled to Haran many miles away. After twenty years and much hardship at the hands of his father-in-law, Jacob returned to his father's land with two wives and eleven children.

He was still afraid to see Esau, but had an encounter with an angel which increased his trust in the Lord. It was after this that Jacob had a visitation from the Lord and his name was changed to Israel. He was to be the father of the 12 sons who would eventually become the 12 tribes of Israel. It took many years for the the deceitful Jacob to change to the more righteous Israel, but God was faithful. His hand never left the man. He will also be faithful to your children if you will continue in your belief and prayer.

Throughout the scriptures, prophets were given words from God which told what He was planning to do. Sometimes there were warnings in an attempt to get people to repent.

Other times He would give words about future times of restoration and reward. These words are for us to know what we
can expect in the future. We might recognize certain things
as they happen, knowing that God has spoken of them. For
instance, throughout the scriptures there were words which
foretold of the Messiah who was to come. Matthew's gospel
account brings out many of those words and how they were
fulfilled in Jesus.

There is another reason for these prophecies. When we
see the promises for God's deliverance, He wants us to pray for
those things to come to pass. We know that His will is for us to
have those good things, so He wants us to ask.

---

*When we see the promises for God's
deliverance, He wants us to pray
for those things to come to pass*

I would like to show you an example of this. In the
book of Daniel, we see a man who was true to his God while
in very difficult circumstances. His nation, Judah, had been
taken into captivity and transported to Babylon. So there he
was in a foreign land, being ruled by heathens.

Even in these dire circumstances, Daniel remained

faithful in prayer and lived a holy life. After many years had passed, he was reading the scriptures, and noticed that Jeremiah had prophesied that the nation would be in captivity for 70 years. And guess what! 70 years had passed! (See Daniel 9:2 and Jeremiah 29:10) So Daniel began to pray this word back to God. Daniel's prayers began the process which brought about the return of the Jews and restoration of Jerusalem. When Daniel saw the promise in the Word, he asked for it, and it happened.

As you read scriptures, you will see the promises your Father has for you. Ask for them. He is faithful to perform His Word. I want to look at a scripture which we saw earlier.

Isaiah 55:10-11

For as the rain and snow come down from heaven,
And do not return there without watering the earth,
And making it bear and sprout,
And furnishing seed to the sower and bread to the eater,
So shall My Word be which goes forth from My mouth
It shall not return to Me empty
Without accomplishing what I desire,
And without succeeding in the matter for which I sent it.

Now we know how God sent his Word. It's the Bible. It's rain and snow. Remember we talked about the snow being the Word as it is written. When it is revealed, or spoken to you, it melts and becomes like beneficial water.

So how does it return to Him? It returns to Him when you pray that Word back to Him. When you ask Him for what He promised. He wants you to pray and ask Him for what He promised, and He will surely do it.

My husband, Mickey, has used the illustration of a desert. The reason the desert is so dry is that there is no water there to evaporate. When water evaporates, it brings rain back to the earth. In areas where there is a large body of water, there is lots of evaporation and lots of rain or snow. (Just ask people who live in the Northeast where they get snow from the Great Lakes. They even call it "Lake-effect Snow.") The evaporation is like prayer. When there is no prayer, or evaporation, then your life is very dry. You don't see God working very much. But if you are full of God's living water and His Word, you will pray (return) that Word back to Him, then the answers

---

He wants the Word to succeed in the matter for which He sent it

---

will shower down upon you. Your life will no longer be a desert, but a lush place.

He wants the Word "to succeed in the matter for which He sent it." That purpose was for us to pray it and have it come to pass.

If your life seems to be "dry," maybe you need to step up your prayer. As you evaporate the Word back to God, through your prayer, you will begin to see the rain of His answers come to your life. He wants to answer your prayer.

I want to share one more thing which will show the significance of asking God. Let's look at the 17th chapter of John. Now if ever in the history of the world there was anyone who was in the perfect will of God, it was Jesus. Right? That goes without saying. He was the Holy Son of God. Perfect. Always doing the will of His Father.

So what does He say?

John 17:1
Father, the time has come.
Now glorify Me as I have glorified You.

Then He goes on to pray for His disciples and for us.

If Jesus lived in God's perfect will - and He did, why would He have to tell God the time has come? Why would He ask for God to glorify Him? Why would He have to pray that God would honor us and keep us? God the Father loves us too. Why was this entire prayer necessary?

It all goes back to the original plan. Because of man's

dominion, a MAN had to pray from earth for that will to be done. In my mind, that was one of the most important missions of Jesus while He was on the earth. God needed a man to pray for us according to His will. That man had to pray that we would be one with Him and would be one with each other. That prayer is loaded with the will of God for His new creations. Praise God, the prayer of Jesus was answered.

When you look in the scriptures and see God's promises, remember, He wants you to ask for those things. That paves the way for Him to accomplish His will for you and for those around you. You open the door for His mighty hand to work!

When you pray according to His will- His Word – you will see Him work in ways which will astound you. He is better than you know!

In closing this chapter, I would like to give you a personal example. When my children were in high school, I would often pray for them in their studies. One scripture which the Lord spoke to me was from Daniel. It is speaking of the Hebrew children, but the Lord said I could claim it for my own. The scripture in Daniel 1:4 says that the Hebrews had "intelligence in every branch of wisdom, and were endowed with understanding, and discerning knowledge." I would take that scripture and ask my Father to do the same for my children.

I would ask Him to give them favor with the teachers and to give them the wisdom they needed. Then I would ask angels to go and hover around them as they took a test or completed an assignment.

Let your Father show you the Words to claim for your own

On occasion, my children would tell me that they had gone into a test with great confusion, afraid they wouldn't do well. As they started to take the test, they would suddenly "know" the answers. The subject matter would become clear.

Your Father will do the same for you. Let Him show you the Words to claim for your own. Then pray them back to Him in faith. He is faithful to perform His Word.

I would like to suggest to you that you buy a prayer journal or notebook. You might keep a record of your prayer needs. Also include the words which you have received from your heavenly Father. These words could be scripture you "noticed" as you read or words which you received in prayer. Then record the answers to your prayers as they come. You will find yourself growing in faith as you see your Father work in your life.

Remember, patience and perseverance are essential in prayer. Things don't necessarily happen over night. But if we continue praying according to the will of God, we will see the desired results.

Let's Go Deeper

1. Read Jeremiah 29:10; Daniel 9:2; II Chronicles 36:21

Do you see how God used Daniel to pray according
to what He had spoken to Jeremiah? Write
your observations about how this works.

2. Read John 17

Does this speak to you for today? Explain.

God Said,
"Let there be light,"
and there
was light.
Genesis 1:3

Chapter Eleven
God Speaks
His Word

We are in deeper water now- water to our loins. Our goal is to improve our ability to pray according to God's plan. We want to be more effective in prayer. So let's get some more clarity about God's plan: what we are calling "the rules of the universe." Let's jump in.

One of the most helpful revelations you will ever have is that our world is run by WORDS. We are such visual people, we think that other things are more important than words, but we are mistaken. The most powerful thing on earth is God's Word!

Look around you and observe. You look up and see the sun, the moon, the stars, and the clouds. You look around and see an abundance of trees, flowers, rocks, and animals. Then you have the mountains, the oceans, the rivers, and all of the topographies of the world. There is so much to see. If you ever have watched Discovery Channel or National Geographic Channel you might be mesmerized by the complexities of nature. What a wonderful testimony to the greatness of God!

So how did He do it? How did it all come to be? God, our Creator, the All-Powerful One SPOKE it into existence. In Genesis 1, He said, "Let there be light" (literally, "Light, be") and light was. He said over and over, "let there be" and "let there be" and everything He called for appeared. God created the world and all that is in it through words. As His Word was spoken, the Holy Spirit, who was hovering over the earth, brought it to pass.

> Hebrews 11:3
>
> *By faith we understand that the worlds were framed by the Word of God so that things which are seen were not made of things that are visible.*

Things we can't see, the Words of God, created the things we see. The worlds were literally made by the Word of God. Please take some time now and think about that. Let God reveal to you the significance of what we are saying. WORDS CREATE THINGS!!

Our minds can't understand how this could work. It is above our understanding, yet it's true. When God's Word is spoken, the Holy Spirit brings His plan to pass.

Now let's go on. Let's read about Jesus entering the earth. We know that He was born of a virgin. So how did

God's seed enter Mary's womb? (Does "seed" give you a clue?) Look with me now.

In Luke 1:31, an angel appeared to Mary and SPOKE to her.

He said, "And, behold, you will conceive and bring forth a Son, and shall call His name Jesus. He will be great, and will be called the Son of the Highest, and the Lord God will give Him the throne of His Father David. And He will reign over the house of Jacob forever."

Then Mary said to the angel, "How can this be, since I do not know a man?"

And the angel answered and said to her, "The Holy Spirit will come upon you, and the power of the Highest will overshadow you. Therefore, also, that Holy One who is to be born will be called the Son of God"…

Then Mary said, "Behold the maidservant of the Lord! Let it be done to me according to your word"

When I read this, I see something really exciting. I see the WORD of GOD being spoken to Mary and her receiving it. Just as in the creation story, when God's Word was spoken and the Holy Spirit hovering over the earth brought it to pass, now I see the Word being spoken, Mary receiving it, and the Holy Spirit bringing it to pass. He hovered over her and performed God's Word just as He did in Genesis.

Jesus was conceived by God's Word. That explains the account in John.

John 1:14

> *"and the Word became flesh and dwelt among us, and we beheld His glory; the glory as of the only begotten of the Father, full of grace and truth."*

Do you see that? The Word became flesh. The Word was spoken to Mary and became flesh – the manifested Son of God, born of His seed, the Word.

Right now I can hear the Twilight Zone music going off in your head. You may be saying, "This is too far out for me. I just want to get my children delivered." But if you will hang in there with me, you will be able to see some things which will cause your prayers to increase in power. Our God loves us and our children. He wants the best for us. If we will honor His Word and His rules, we will see miracles performed within our own families.

Once your eyes are opened to the power of God's Word, you see it again and again. Look at the following scriptures.

John 1:1-3

In the beginning was the Word
and the Word was with God and the Word was God....
All things were made through Him,
and without Him nothing was made that was made.

Hebrews 1:2,3

God has in these last days spoken to us by His Son,
whom He has appointed heir of all things, through
whom also He made the worlds, who being the bright-
ness of His glory and the express image of His person,
and UPHOLDING ALL THINGS BY THE
WORD OF HIS POWER.

The power of the Word of God not only created everything we see, but that power is also keeping everything in place. It upholds all things. The earth, the heavens, the seasons, all continue to operate by the power from that spoken Word. Wow!

When you look at the ministry of Jesus you see the power of His Word again and again. How did He raise Lazarus from the dead? He SAID, "Lazarus, come forth."(John 11:43) When He stilled the storm He SAID, "Peace. Be still!" (Mark 4:39) There was power in his words. He ruled through words.

One day, as I was praying for one of my children, the

Lord spoke to me. He said, "If Jesus were to appear in the flesh again, come to your house, and take care of your problem, He would do it through words." "Be healed!" "Rise up!" "Stand up!" "Come forth!" There were many times when He would lay hands on people or touch them to transfer His anointing, but most of the time, He brought the deliverance just by speaking the Word.

Angels obey the voice of His Word

Now it's our turn! We are born again, restored children of God. We are Word people also! Earlier we talked about the Word as seed being planted and germinating in our hearts. The Word was to produce a crop, just as natural seeds do. Well now it's time to talk about what type of crop it produces.

The Word first of all brings us closer to our Father. It brings us faith in His goodness and His love for us. It changes our selfish way of thinking to His way of thinking. It also shows us His will. Yet there is more.

The Word, when it is filled with faith, coming from our lips, becomes our method of ruling in our lives. Remember we said we were to rule and reign in our sphere? Well a significant part of our ruling is done through the words we speak. When we believe God's Word and speak it, things happen. Demons have to flee. "Angels obey the voice of His Word." (Psalm 103:20) This is what we call "decreeing" the Word or "prophesying" the Word.

Many years ago my husband and I were praying about some problems our teenagers had encountered. We were both in distress over some bad influences which were trying to prevail. (When you are in distress, your faith level isn't very high). As we prayed, Mickey had a vision. He saw a team of angels sitting in a box similar to what you see in hockey games. The angels were looking at him intently. As my husband saw them, he knew that they were waiting for the Word. They were waiting to obey the voice of God's Word. The angels were leaning forward, as if to show their eagerness to "get into the game." Accompanied with the scripture in Psalm 103:20, Mickey and I had a greater understanding of our part in speaking God's Word.

Taking the cue, Mickey began to say, "It is written...," just as Jesus did as He spoke God's Word into the atmosphere. As Mickey spoke, he saw the angels leap out of the box and into action. Thousands of mighty angels were at work on our behalf. Soon afterwards we began to see the results surrounding our children.

Jesus often charged His disciples (and that's us) that what they said was important.

Mark 11:23-24

Have faith in God.

Truly I say to you, whoever SAYS to this mountain, "Be taken up and cast into the sea." And does not doubt in his heart, but believes that what he SAYS is going to happen, it shall be granted him.

Therefore, I say to you, all things for which you pray and ask, believe that you received them, and they shall be granted you.

In this passage, Jesus is talking about faith, but He is also talking about words. "If you SAY." "Believe what you SAY." When God's Words are read and valued they are revealed to you and your faith rises. Then as you speak them out, you help bring about God's plan – His very good, loving plan into your life and the lives of your children.

Now let's be clear. When Jesus spoke, His words were immediately creative. The world was created. The fig tree dried up. The wind stopped. I don't have to remind you that you and I don't operate to that degree of faith and power. However, if you will be persistent in speaking God's Word, you will see changes in the right direction.

Remember Harvey and June Lancet we met in the first chapter? She had been healed from cancer and they were born again, but they still had problems with their sons who were on drugs. When we talked about the Lancets the first time, you may have thought that their speaking the Word and praying the Word seemed strange. Well, now that we have seen more of God's plan, let's take a look at them again.

As the two studied God's Word and prayed everyday, the Lord would quicken certain verses to them. What stood out to June was Proverbs 6:31

When the thief gets caught, he must repay seven times.

Harvey had another verse which God had given him. Isaiah 54:13

All of your sons will be disciples, taught of the Lord

When Harvey and June began to understand the subject we are talking about right now - that God wanted them to pray that Word back to Him and to declare the Word to the atmosphere around them - they were obedient to do what He said. They prayed and prophesied, prayed and prophesied - day in and day out.

Just before the two sons were sent to prison, a mutual

friend was visiting them. While she was there, a policeman called to tell the father that the sons had been arrested again and were being held in jail. What did the father reply to the policeman? Did he say, "Well those boys will never amount to anything?" No. The father very calmly replied in the phone to the policeman, "Well, my sons are disciples, taught of the Lord." Now the policeman may have thought the father was crazy, but Harvey wasn't trying to impress the officer. He was trying to bring deliverance to his sons. He was determined that he would not agree with the devil and what he was trying to accomplish. He was going to agree with God and what He said.

Sometimes it looked hard, but we never gave up

Years later when I saw June and got the good report about Ken and Martin, she was jubilant about God's wonderful plan. "We never gave up," she said. "Sometimes it was very hard. It looked impossible. Yet we knew that God's Word was true. We were determined to see that Word manifested in our family!" And they did!

Over the years there have been countless times when I have used this very concept in praying for my children. The devil will try to bring fear, worry, or doubt to you concerning your children. But you must resist that at all costs. Agree with God. Believe what God says. Say what God says.

As you speak what God says, you are hearing that Word as you speak it. So your faith is rising. Then you say it more, and your faith rises more. As you continue that process, your faith increases and the power of your words increases. It's like an upward spiral which carries you into greater blessings.

There is creative, supernatural power in God's Word. When you let His will, His Word, become part of you, you grow in faith and confidence as you speak His Word. In this way, we work with Him. Because of man's dominion on the earth, there are certain things He chooses to have done from earth. (Remember, it's His plan. He designed it this way). One of those things is the speaking of His Word. So do it! Pray God's Word and speak God's Word as He directs. You will see Him at work on your behalf!

Let's Go Deeper

1. Read Luke 7:1-10

Why did the centurian say that Jesus only had to "speak the word?"

Why did Jesus remark on his faith?

2. Read Psalm 103:20

Think about the angels obeying the voice of God's word?

Who gives "voice" to God's Word?

He who believes
in Me,
as the scripture said,
"From
his innermost being
shall flow rivers
of living water."
John 7:38

Chapter Twelve
Holy Spirit Power

Take a deep breath now. We are about to go a little deeper. We are going to yield ourselves totally to the Holy Spirit. We belong to Him – and it's time to let Him have His way!

As you've read this book, you may have noticed that much of what I have shared has been based on personal experience. That's one of the major ways the Lord has trained me. He would bring me an experience – and then He would show me in the Bible – usually something that I had never seen before.

Well, here we go again. After I committed my life to the Lord in 1979, my prayer life increased. Very often, after my children were asleep, I would spend time praying and reading the Word. One night as I was praying out loud, something very different happened. I began to babble in what seemed like a primitive language. I was shocked! I had heard of others having that experience, so I knew what it was. I was praying in "tongues." Some people call it "receiving their prayer language." I had been baptized with the Holy Spirit! It was mind boggling to me at that time!

Now many people will use glowing terms when they tell about their first encounter with the Holy Spirit. They will make it sound like they had entered into the heavenlies for an experience. I'm sure that happens to some, but not to me. In fact, it scared me.

I had never heard anyone pray in tongues, so I didn't know what it might sound like. I knew that the disciples in the Book of Acts had spoken in other languages. But that was then; and this was now! I knew that I had been under a lot of pressure, and I was a little afraid that I was "losing it!"

I told no one of the experience and decided that I definitely did not want that! About three months passed. Then one night a dear friend came to visit. We were sharing the Word, when I mentioned my encounter. I told her that the experience was definitely not for me! She looked amazed.

Cathy then told me that she, too, had her "prayer language," as she called it. She also said, "It's such a wonderful gift from God. I can't believe that you have received it and don't want it!" As my friend continued to share her experience, something began to stir in my heart.

That night, after my friend left, I sat on my sofa and lifted my hands to God. I said, "Lord, I don't understand what was happening, but if this can help me, I want it. I want everything You have for me." As I sat in the stillness, my prayer was answered. I began praying in tongues.

This time was different. After my friend had helped build my confidence, I yielded to the Holy Spirit. What happened next was somewhat of a test. (Our Lord is so ready to take us to the next level, He will overlook our errors if our hearts are right).

There were two personal problems which were bothering me. While going through my divorce a few years before, I had started smoking and very quickly had become addicted. I had wanted to quit the habit, but grave physical symptoms had emerged every time I had tried to stop. On this special night, I held up my hands and said, "I want to quit smoking," and then babbled in tongues.

The second problem concerned a daughter who was going through the "sixth grade nya-nya's." (Mothers will understand this). A couple of her friends had ganged up and were hurting her feelings. So I held up my daughter's name and repeated the process.

What followed was astounding. First, I decided to try to quit smoking on Saturday - two days away. On that Saturday morning I awoke a non-smoker. I had no desire for a cigarette and I had no withdrawal symptoms. There was no weight gain, no headaches, no dizzy spells. It was totally supernatural, as only I could know.

Then, as for my daughter, she came to me three days later and asked for me to pray with her. She wanted to receive Jesus as her Savior. Needless to say, I was ecstatic! In fact, as an added benefit, a second daughter came running in to receive Him also. Our family was being transformed.

Once you have seen the results of your prayer, no one can talk you out of it

---

Now there were people who would come to me after this and have theories, supposedly out of the Word, denouncing my experience. But there is an old saying: "The person with an experience will never be at the mercy of the person with a theory." Once you have personally tasted God's goodness as He prays through you in an unknown language, and once you have seen some of the results, no one can ever talk you out of it. In fact, from that very early experience, I was sold on praying in tongues! I had just entered into a new realm of God's glory.

Just as in my other encounters, God began to confirm my experience in His Word. He showed me in I Corinthians 14:18 where Paul discusses "praying in tongues" or "praying in the Spirit." He says that he is glad that he prays in tongues more than any of the others. Why would that be? He must find it beneficial.

In the same chapter Paul says that if anyone prays in tongues, he "edifies himself." (I Corinthians 14:4) That means he builds himself up in the spirit. He brings enlightenment to himself. He increases his ability to understand God's Word as the Holy Spirit is praying through him. He also can hear God's voice more clearly.

Paul mentions another benefit of praying in tongues in Jude 20. He says when you pray in tongues, or in the Spirit, you build yourself up on your most holy faith. Your faith increases. You are increasing your ability to see what your Father wants you to see, and to believe what your Father wants you to believe.

Soon after I started my newest adventure with God, I had many confirmations that I was on the right track. I prayed for myself and I prayed for my children. I saw them overcome many obstacles and grow in their knowledge of God. I also was growing in my relationship with my Lord.

One day as I was driving in my car, I was praying in tongues – with no understanding. My work required some travel, so I had been driving for about two hours - driving and praying - just building myself up. I had no idea as to what I was praying. After work, I stopped at a grocery store and happened to see a lady I hadn't seen for awhile. We chatted briefly and went on our way. As I was leaving the store, the Holy Spirit spoke to me. He said, "Alice has received her prayer language, and I want you to talk to her about it." I happened to know that Alice attended a church whose pastor was very opposed to tongues. He had a television program, and I had heard him publicly denounce the experience of tongues. So, I hesitated and went on to my car. Suddenly a strong voice began speaking to my spirit, "GO AND TALK TO HER!"

As I shyly approached Alice, I asked where she was going to church – and I was right. It was the church which taught against the experience. Determined to be obedient, with all the courage I could muster, I blurted out, "Do you have the baptism in the Holy Spirit?"

You should have seen her face! "How did you know?!

No one knows! How did you know?! How did you know?!"
She almost screamed the words. She went on, "My husband
doesn't believe in tongues and would be very upset. How did
you know?!" At this point it was very clear that the Lord wanted to encourage Alice in her new experience. As we chatted, we
both were encouraged and so in awe of the goodness of God.

Would I have heard the voice of the Holy Spirit if I
hadn't been praying in tongues? I don't think so. As I was praying in tongues, I was becoming more sensitive to His voice.
When He had an assignment for me, I could clearly hear Him.
Just as it mentions in I Corinthians 14:4, I had been edifying
myself! As I was built up in the Spirit, I could hear Him.

So how does all of this apply to our prayers for our
children? That is my favorite part. Of course, we want to hear
clearly from the Spirit about the specific prayers we need to
make. But there is more.

Almost every Christian knows Romans 8:28
*He causes all things to work together for the good of
those who love the Lord and who are called according
to His purpose.*

That verse is one we take out of context and apply
to any occasion. Remember the satellite approach? Let's use
it now to take a look at the full message. Let's put that puzzle

piece back where it belongs and see what the Holy Spirit was really saying.

> Romans 8: 26-28
>
> *And in the same way the Spirit also helps our weakness; for we do not know how to pray as we should, but the Spirit Himself intercedes for us with groanings too deep for words;*
>
> *And He who searches the hearts knows what the mind of the Spirit is, because He intercedes for the saints according to the will of God.*
>
> *And we know that God causes all things to work together for good to those who love God, to those who are called according to His purpose.*

If you are very familiar with this verse, you may have a hard time even seeing its meaning in context. If that is so, please spend some time meditating on these verses so that the truth can come into focus. The Holy Spirit speaking to us through Paul didn't jump around from subject to subject – throwing out all sorts of ideas. He was speaking to us about one very important subject: praying in tongues (with groanings too deep for words – not in our own language).

So what does the Holy Spirit say? He says

The Holy Spirit

- Knows the mind of the Spirit (His will)
- Knows the hearts (our will)
- Prays according to the perfect will of God
  (according to our covenant)

  And in that way He is causing all things to work together for the good of us and our children.

As we pray in tongues (or the Spirit), God's perfect plan comes into reality. We are praying God's perfect will – which is always good. Even when we don't know what we are praying, we can KNOW that the Spirit is praying according to the perfect will of God - making all things work together for our good – and the good of those for whom we are praying.

We are praying God's will which is always good

Can you even imagine how significant this is when you are praying for your children? This gift is a wonderful treasure! When we realize that the world was formed by God's Word, Jesus was conceived by God's Word, and God runs things by His Word, how magnificent it is that He has put His supernatural Words in our mouths for us to bring about His plans in our lives. I pray that you never despise or take lightly this wonderful gift!

There are many times when we do not know how to pray for our children. As our children grow up and spend more time away from us, this is so significant! We don't know everything that is happening around them. We don't even know what kinds of temptations they may be having. We don't know what they are doing or thinking. Yet the Holy Spirit does. As we yield to His prayers, we can see the fruit of our labors.

I am not saying that these prayers will control your children. GOD HAS GIVEN THEM FREE WILL. However, there will be times when your prayers in the Spirit will push back the forces of darkness and help them to make the right decisions. There may be times when they aren't listening and they fall into a ditch. Even in those cases God's special prayers can bring deliverance. There are times when your prayers in the Spirit will keep your children protected.

In my personal life, praying in tongues for my children has been a huge part of my prayer life. There have been many times when the Lord would wake me in the middle of the night. I would know that He was calling me to pray for one of my children. They might have been living in another town and I might not have known what was going on that day, but I would pray in the Spirit until I felt peace in my spirit. Sometimes I would find out what I was praying for. Sometimes I wouldn't. Yet over the years I have seen many benefits from these prayers and I have seen God's love holding onto my children.

I will give you some examples. A few years ago, I awoke in the middle of the night and felt a call to pray for my pregnant daughter. Not knowing the circumstances, I prayed in the Spirit. The call continued throughout the night and into the next day. I had other obligations, but even as I drove or worked, I quietly prayed in tongues. Then I received a call. My daughter had gone into labor. It was three weeks early, but her first baby had been early.

I hurried to Atlanta to be with her. Her labor started and then it stopped. Nothing seemed to be happening and the baby was showing signs of distress. The doctor said that if something didn't happen soon, she would have to have a Caeserian section. I went out into the hall of the hospital and continued to pray. Suddenly, labor resumed, and a healthy baby was born. I am not saying that I was the only one praying or that my prayers alone brought the result. But I am saying that my prayers HELPED bring God's best for my daughter and grandson!

Amanda was a mother whose daughter, Olivia, was anorexic. She had compared herself with pencil-thin models so often that she no longer saw herself as she was. Olivia was beautiful, but she was getting dangerously thin. Yet when she looked in the mirror, she saw an overweight person. After several years of this, with yo-yo dieting, bulimia, and many tears, Olivia's health was in grave danger. She would be hospitalized, but as soon as she was released, the downward spiral would continue. Olivia was 5'7" and weighed less than 100 pounds. Strangely, she still saw herself as fat! Amanda had spent many hours in prayer, but Olivia, now in college, seemed totally indifferent to her problem.

One night at 3:00 AM Amanda awoke with a start. She was suddenly wide awake and felt the Holy Spirit calling her to pray. As Amanda walked into her den, she felt an urge to "pray in tongues" – not knowing why.

He says,"Now! Go! Let's get this job done!"

For the next three days Amanda spent most of the time praying in tongues. She had other obligations which required her to be around people, so she would quietly pray under her breath. Then as soon as she was alone, she would yield to the Spirit and pray more intensely. During that time, this mother lost her appetite completely. Her entire focus was on praying in tongues.

After three days, Amanda felt the prayer assignment lift and she continued with her normal routine – still unaware of the reason for her prayer. On day five, she had an amazing thrill! Olivia called in tears. She had suddenly become aware of her condition and had checked herself into the hospital. She was ready to receive the help she so desperately needed. Within weeks, Amanda's precious daughter, Olivia, was well on her way to recovery.

As she shared her story with me, Amanda said, "I never knew what I was praying for, but the Holy Spirit did. He prayed for my Olivia according to God's perfect will – and deliverance was sure to come."

Why didn't that happen sooner? Of course, I don't know all the answers, but I believe that God waited until Olivia's will was at a place of softening, a place where she was willing to let the Lord speak to her. When someone's heart is hard, they won't listen to anyone – including the voice of God. But the Lord knows just how to continue to work with people, bringing them opportunities, until they are willing to listen. It's as if one day He says, "Now! Go! The time is right! Let's get this job done!"

Over the years, I have had many experiences of being called into prayer for my children. My own children have later shared dangerous situations they encountered – or times of testing. Often they never knew I was praying for them, but time and again I have seen the Holy Spirit praying God's will – and causing things to work together for the good of my own children.

Our Father is so amazing! Earlier we discussed God's Word and its power. We saw how God's Word in faith-filled lips can commission angels, stop demons, and bring about God's will in our lives. Doesn't it make sense that He would provide His own language to His children so that they could bring about His will? What a miracle we have in God's marvelous plan!

What a miracle we have in God's marvelous plan

Right now is a very significant time for you. I want you to think about what we have just talked about. Do you have the baptism in the Holy Spirit – with evidence of praying in tongues? If so, never take it lightly or despise it. Never be ashamed of your precious Holy Spirit. He is your best friend in the earth. The greatest miracle of all is that the Holy Spirit knows you better than you know yourself. He knows every mistake, every flaw, every hurt, every disappointment, every desire. And He loves you more than you can even understand. He loves you more than anyone on earth is capable of loving you.

Lift up your hands to Jesus and pray for more of His Spirit to manifest in your life. Yield to the Holy Spirit and pray in your heavenly prayer language. Know that as you pray in tongues, you are building up your faith and your ability to hear His voice. Know also that you are praying His perfect, wonderful will into existence.

If you have never received your prayer language, you may be a little nervous about this. I understand. If you have grown up in a traditional church, you may have even heard doctrine that says the gifts are not for today. It's interesting, however, that I have never heard anyone who has truly received and yielded to this manifestation say it's not for today.

There is also confusion which comes because of misunderstanding I Corinthians 14. In that chapter, Paul mentions that in church, if one speaks in tongues, there needs to be an interpretation. Well, that passage is talking about people speaking out in church, giving a message to the congregation. Needless to say, other people won't get the message if you just speak in tongues with no interpretation. I am talking about something else here. I am talking about praying in the spirit, in an unknown tongue. I am talking about praying God's perfect will by the power of the Holy Spirit. Sometimes you will know what you are praying; sometimes you won't. Your Father wants to bless you with all that He has. If you desire to be filled with the Holy Spirit, He will do it.

> Luke 11:9-13 Jesus says:
>
> *And I say to you, ask, and it shall be given to you; seek, and you shall find; knock, and it shall be opened to you.*
>
> *For everyone who asks, receives; and he who seeks, finds; and to him who knocks, it shall be opened.*
>
> *Now suppose one of you fathers is asked by his son for a fish; he will not give him a snake instead of a fish, will he?*
>
> *Or if he is asked for an egg, he will not give him a scorpion, will he?*
>
> *If you, then, being evil, know how to give good gifts to your children, how much more shall your heavenly Father give the Holy Spirit to those who ask Him.*

See what He says? You don't have to be concerned that your Father will withhold from you. Neither do you need to be concerned that your "unknown language" will be saying things harmful. You can have faith that your God is a loving God. He wants only the best for you. You can rest in the assurance that when you ask, seek, and knock for God's best, He will give it to you. If you want more of God's power in your life, ask Him to fill you. You have nothing to lose in trying. You will be amazed at the increase of power you will experience.

There are several ways to receive the baptism in the Holy Spirit. If you know some Spirit-filled believers you may ask them to pray with you to receive. Or you may want to spend time with your heavenly Father in the privacy of your home and ask Him for it. Either way, I encourage you to receive all that your Father has for you. Your prayers will enter into a new realm as you do!

I pray now that you receive the Holy Spirit and your prayer language. I also pray that when you have received it, you not take Him lightly, but that you pray in tongues a lot! He has many wonderful things He wants to show you! He also has many great things He wants to accomplish in your life.

There will be times when you will know what you are praying about and even have some understanding about what you are saying. Other times you won't. Just trust your Heavenly Father. As you receive your own prayer language and begin to pray in that way, you will have your own testimony of the many marvelous answers which you will receive.

Let's Go Deeper

1. Read Acts 2:1-40

   Let the Lord speak to you about this great
   manifestation which came to the earth.

   Think about Peter and how bold he was. Then read
   Matthew 26:69-75 Do you see the power that
   came to Peter after he received the Holy spirit?

2. Read Acts 19:1-6

   Write your personal observations
   about this passage.

*I am
the Alpha
and the Omega,
says the Lord God,
who is and who was
and who is to come,
the Almighty*
Revelation 1:8

Chapter Thirteen
Putting It All Together

We've covered a lot of territory. We've talked about being born again, being filled with the Spirit, and honoring God's Word as final authority and as absolute truth. We've also talked about praying God's Word back to Him and speaking (or decreeing) His Word into the earth. Then in the last chapter, we talked about praying in the Spirit, or "unknown tongues." Wow! That's a lot of information.

So now you might be saying, "How do I use all of this information? When do I pray to God? When do I speak His Word? When do I pray in tongues?" Well to answer these questions, we must get back to our very first thoughts. We are sold out to God. We belong to Him. We are committed to Him. So He is our Leader in prayer.

You are not a parrot! You don't just chatter words of scripture with no faith and expect things to happen. Neither are you a copycat! Our Father wants a unique, authentic relationship with each of us. We are His children and every aspect of our walk begins there. We don't just take steps one, two, and three. We don't just copy someone else's prayer life or their words. We pray and prophesy the scriptures which speak to us personally.

When you listen to people share their walk of prayer, they may sound very different in the way they approach things. However, the principles are the same. God speaks to them in their inner man, and He directs their prayer.

God speaks to them in their inner man, and He directs their prayer

---

I'll share with you how I go about my prayer. (But this is just an example. Remember, your Father wants to direct you personally). I start with worshipping and praising my Lord. I thank Him for who He is and for His wonderful plan for me and my loved ones. I read His Word for awhile. Then I begin to listen. Sometimes I will pray in the Holy Spirit for awhile. I keep my Bible handy so that my Father can give me some scripture. He will impress upon me something or someone to pray for. At times He will show me something to pray to Him. Sometimes He will impress upon me some words to decree into the atmosphere. Each prayer session is different.

As you can see, the prayer session is directed by my Lord. He is the boss. He knows what is good for me and for my family. He tells me what to pray and when to pray it. It's truly a supernatural walk of faith which allows me to work with my God to achieve His purposes. What a privilege!

In short, He NEEDS someone to pray because of the way He set up His plan. I NEED Him to carry out His plan. I have the dominion on earth. He has the power to make it happen. The two of us work together and His will gets accomplished.

So Let's Review:

• Jesus paid the price for us to be born again of the Spirit of God. Now we have the Holy Spirit living inside of us.

• God's Word, the Bible, is His Word to us. The Holy Spirit will take the Word and reveal it to us. As we meditate on it, we will have greater understanding of God and His ways.

• God has given man dominion on the earth. We are not puppets. We have free will. Therefore, He wants someone to ask Him for His Word to be accomplished.

• Sometimes we see something in the Word which is not happening and we ask our God for it.

• Sometimes we see something in the Word and we make that decree into the earth. When we do, angels and demons obey that Word.

• Sometimes we do not know how to pray and we pray in other tongues, knowing that God's perfect will is being carried out.

• Our prayers are being directed by our Father as we listen to Him and are obedient to Him. We are working with Him to accomplish His purpose.

Esther was a mother of two teenagers. One was committed to the Lord and the other was not. She prayed for them both, but her prayers would be very different. For Jake, the committed one, the Lord might show Esther challenges that were looming on the horizon. Perhaps he needed extra strength to withstand a temptation. Or maybe he needed to have his confidence increased. In those cases, Esther would find the scripture which would address those issues. Maybe:

Ephesians 3:16 and 6:10

Lord, let Jake be "*strengthened with power through your Spirit in his inner man.*" or "Lord, make Jake *strong in the Lord and in the power of Your might."*

For Deborah, the wandering one, her prayers would be different. For her, the Lord might say to pray

Ephesians 1:18 and Colossians 1:9

"Lord, *enlighten the eyes of Deborah's heart so that she may know the hope of Your calling. Father, give her the ear of a disciple: let her hear You. Fill her with a knowledge of Your will in all wisdom and understanding so that she may walk in a way that pleases You."*

These are examples. But they are the types of things that real people are dealing with. Marge had a teenage daughter, Jackie, who went through a "the less work the better" stage. (I'm sure you know what I mean.) One of her teachers called Marge in for a conference. It was clear from the meeting that the teacher was very annoyed with Jackie. She had been disrupting class with her jokes, was not doing her work, and her grades were suffering.

Marge went to the Lord and got the wisdom. First, she needed to help Jackie see that her behavior was wrong. Through her counsel and prayer, Marge brought her daughter to that place and Jackie repented for her mistakes. Then, the Lord gave her some scripture.

Psalm 91:14,15

He will be with me in trouble. He will deliver me and

honor me. He will set me securely on high.

Marge and Jackie began to pray those verses. They knew that what Jackie had done was wrong. Now that she had repented, they were asking God to deliver her from the wrath of her teacher. It was clear that some work needed to be done in the heart of the teacher for Jackie to be able to have a successful year.

A few months passed and Marge saw the teacher at a PTA meeting. Stopping Marge in the hall, the instructor said, "I have never seen anyone change so much so fast! Jackie is doing great!" The Lord had been working- not only on the daughter's heart, but on the teacher's also. One more victory!

Now let's add something to what we have said so far. When we were born again, we were not born to be wimps. We were born strong - in His strength. That means that when answers don't come quickly, we don't quit. If we know that we are praying God's will, we never give up! We keep on going.

There are scriptures which confirm this strength.

II Corinthians 10:3,4

For though we walk in the flesh, we do not war according to the flesh, but the weapons of our warfare are powerful for the destruction of fortresses.

Our weapons are powerful! We are the stong ones. Then in

Ephesians 6:17

Take the helmet of salvation and the sword of the Spirit,
which is the Word of God.

The Word of God is a weapon which we use against the devil and his plans. It is powerful and effective. As you take the scriptures which you know are God's will, you must speak them with conviction and force. Do you see why we are called "prayer warriors?"

I'm sure many people would be surprised to hear how I sound when I am alone. I walk around my house getting tough with the devil - speaking the Word with boldness. I sometimes say in a loud voice, "It is written" and speak some scripture which the Lord has given to me. (Just as Jesus did when He was being tempted by the devil) Luke 4:4.

Thoughts will come into your mind saying that you are wasting your time. Then the circumstances will pop into your mind, and it will look impossible. That is not God's voice. Just get louder and tougher. You are ruling. You are taking dominion over the devil. You win!

Sometimes your prayers will be for seemingly small things, sometimes for big ones. Just keep praying. Whatever the circumstance, keep praying and expect results. Be consistent and persistent. You will see great things accomplished in your family!

Let's Go Deeper

Now is a good time to take a break from reading and spend some time with your Father. Let Him speak to your heart and show you some of these things we've discussed.

Write down in a journal the things He is showing you.

Section Four

...and he led me to a river that I could not ford, for the water had risen...

God
is opposed
to the proud,
but gives grace
to the humble
James 4:6

Chapter Fourteen

Some Life Lessons

Now we are in the deepest water – the water where you swim. We have continued to wade out into the deep until we are now in water over our heads. Our feet don't touch bottom anymore; we can't walk around in our own strength anymore. We have to trust in the Holy Spirit who is holding us up and taking us where He wants us to go. This may seem scary, but it is the best place to be! Remember, this is where the fruit trees grow. It's also where there is an abundance of healing.

This is the place where we truly belong to Jesus – spirit, soul, and body. He is our Lord. He is the boss. In this place we partake of His love in a greater way. We undertake His plans and purposes. He encourages us. He instructs us. He corrects us... Uh-oh! Not that! Yes, that. Whom the Lord loves, He corrects (Hebrews 12:7, 8).

John 15:1-2

I am the true vine, and My Father is the vinedresser.

Every branch in Me that does not bear fruit, He takes away; and every branch that bears fruit, He prunes it, that it may bear more fruit.

We are bearing fruit, so He prunes us. He brings us correction so that we may bear more fruit. He speaks to us about error in our lives. Error only hurts us, and He wants us to be happy and productive.

He brings us correction so that we will bear more fruit

In Joshua 7 there is a great life lesson. Joshua had finally led the sons of Israel across the Jordan River and into the Promised Land. They had circumcised the males and had sworn their commitment to God. Then they, through supernatural intervention of the Most High, had been able to take Jericho – a huge, fortified city.

Things were going great for the Israelites. Then suddenly they had a shocking defeat! They were supposed to take a small town, Ai. The town had only a few people, so Israel's spies advised that only a small number of troops were needed for the mission. But the men of Ai struck down some of Joshua's troops and ran the rest of them away in fear and defeat. Joshua was devastated!

He went before the Lord to inquire of the reasons they were defeated. The answer: there was sin in the camp. When the men had taken Jericho, they were told not to take away any of the spoils. Yet one man, Achan, had secretly taken a Babylonian garment and a few pieces of silver. He had dug a hole in the center of his tent and had buried the items. Covering the items with a rug, Achan thought no one would ever know what he had done. It seemed to be so insignificant. However, God knew and He was very displeased. He notified Joshua that if there was sin in the camp – even if it was secret- they would not be able to stand against their enemies.

The Lord dealt very harshly with Achan so that the Israelites would learn a lesson. When there is sin in the camp, don't expect victory. Thousands of years have passed since that episode, and we now stand under a different covenant. Yet our universe still runs by the same rules. When you have sin in your life – even if you think it is a secret- you can't win over your enemy, Satan.

If you are a Christian mother praying for your children, you probably don't have overt sin with which you are dealing. (If you do, you need to take care of that). The sin I will be addressing is mostly the sin of the heart – the secret sin that we want to justify. Humans have an incredible ability to magnify what their neighbor is doing wrong, while minimizing their own errors. All of us can fall into that trap if we aren't careful. But if we do, we are only deceiving ourselves.

I want you to read the next section very prayerfully. The enemy of our soul, Satan, has an uncanny way of trying to sway our attitudes. He knows that if we are obeying him, he can continue with his tricks on our families. So he tries to drop thoughts into our minds which are contrary to our God, but which are very prevalent in culture. These thoughts, if allowed to grow within us, will give birth to very sinful attitudes. The wrong attitudes, in turn, will hinder our faith and our prayers. If you allow the Holy Spirit to search your heart during this next section, He will begin to shine His light on your darkness and uncover any Babylonian garments you may have hidden in your tent.

First, we have to take our children off the throne of our hearts. Sometimes mothers treat their children like idols. Jesus should have first place in our hearts, not our children. Actually, when we put Jesus on the throne, we really love our children more than ever. But they aren't idols. They are humans and they need Jesus just like anyone else.

When we try to accomplish God's plan from our natural perspective, we always tackle the problem from selfishness and conceit. We think we are better than others. We try to justify ourselves and our children. When our children are in conflicts, we want "ours" to be right and "the others" to be wrong. We justify and then we cover – often times even going into denial.

You have to take your children off the throne of your heart

Let me explain. There was a Christian mother I once knew whose daughter had married a fine Christian man. The two young ones had been college sweethearts and seemed very much in love. During the first years of their lives together, they seemed very happy as they pursued their careers and began their family. From the outside people may have thought this was a wonderful relationship. However, it had to be obvious to the mother that the home was not being built upon the Rock of Jesus. Though the young husband and wife had been raised in Christian homes, Jesus definitely did not have first place in their lives. Materialism was king.

Then the unthinkable happened. The wife, Rachel,

now the mother of two sons and a daughter, discovered that her husband had been living a double life for several years. He traveled often and had a mistress in another city. The news brought nothing but shock to everyone involved. It was obvious that the two had been worldly in their endeavors, but no one had expected such gross misconduct. The mother was devastated – as was Rachel.

For several months, the young pair tried to reconcile. But the hurt went too deep and there were indications that the husband was continuing his affair. The marriage finally ended in divorce.

Leah was the daughter's mother and she spoke with me often during those months. She knew that the answer was with Jesus. She also knew that her prayers could heal her daughter's hurts and change her life. Yet she just couldn't seem to find the breakthrough.

As the distraught mother sobbed before me one day, the Lord shined a light in her heart. Leah began to see through God's eyes. She saw the anger that she had toward her son-in-law and she saw that her attitude was totally biased. Though what the young father had done was inexcusable, her daughter had faults of her own, and those faults needed to be addressed. As humility set in, the burden lifted from Leah's shoulders. Forgiveness, peace, and hope began to arise. She was ready to pray with faith.

Many years have passed since this story took place. God has moved mightily in the life of Leah's daughter and her grandchildren. They have grown closer to the Lord. Rachel has remarried a fine Christian man and they together are prospering in a healthy, God-centered relationship.

There is a wonderful liberty we receive when we are not trying to be seen of men

---

The turning pointed came when Leah humbled herself in her prayers. When she began to face her own shortcomings as well as those of her daughter, her prayers began to prevail. A great paradox in the Christian walk is that when we see ourselves as "great ones" before God, pride can be our downfall. He resists the proud. When we find ourselves excusing ourselves and judging others, we are in trouble. We can expect resistance from the Heavenlies.

There is a wonderful liberty we receive when we are not trying to be seen of men. We are not putting on a mask for others to honor. Our honor comes from our Father who sees in secret. The One who can make the difference in our circumstances knows who we really are anyway. Why do we try to hide the truth from Him? When we let go of our pride, we are truly lifted up.

After Jesus encountered the rich young ruler in Mark 10, He said something so profound that it should be a message to everyone in the modern world.

> Mark 10: 23-27
>
> *And Jesus, looking around, said to His disciples, "How hard it will be for those who are wealthy to enter the kingdom of God!"*
>
> *And the disciples were amazed at His words. But Jesus answered again and said to them, "Children, how hard it is to enter the kingdom of God! It is easier for a camel to go through the eye of a needle than for a rich man to enter the kingdom of God."*
>
> *And they were even more astonished and said to Him, "Then who can be saved?"*
>
> *Looking upon them, Jesus said, "With men it is impossible, but not with God; for all things are possible with God."*

Let's take a look at the "eye of the needle." What did Jesus mean? Many Bible scholars see this in an interesting way. The doors in the walls around Jerusalem, had smaller doors within them. These short, narrow entry points may have been called the "eyes of the needle." When merchants came to the city bringing their wares, the camels had to be stripped down and slid through these entries on their knees. These openings were just large enough for the bare-backed camels to enter. The purpose was to prevent dangerous items from being smuggled into the city. When the camels were stripped, the goods could be examined to be proven secure before they were allowed in.

So what does that have to do with us? We all come into the kingdom of God the same way – repentant and humble. Whether we are rich or poor, old or young, educated or not, we all come to God the same way. We have to become like the bare-backed camels. We have to strip down and take off all of the prideful wares we carry around. We come with just our hearts, soft and pliable in His hands. We don't come bragging on our accomplishments, our riches, or even our own goodness. We strip down and come to Him knowing that we need a Savior just like every other human being from every walk of life.

This attitude is hard for people who are "rich." Whether our riches are from material things or from our achievements we often depend upon them for our identity. We see ourselves as "above" others who haven't achieved that much. This prideful attitude is an abomination to God. How can we love others and still have such haughty vision? We can't!

Unfortunately, the American church is full of haughty people. We are often like the Laodicean church Jesus rebuked.

Revelation 3: 16,17

So because you are lukewarm, and neither hot nor cold, I will spit you out of My mouth. Because you say, "I am rich, and have become wealthy, and have need of nothing." And you do not know that you are wretched and miserable and poor and blind and naked.

Part of this mindset is that we are "proud" of our children. Of course, it's only right that they bring us great joy when they are living good, productive lives. Yet they can become like trophies we display on a mantle, representing to the world that we are good parents. We can glory and boast in their successes, making ourselves look better.

When parents get caught in this trap, they don't want to face the problems which might arise in their offspring. They would rather gloss everything over, shift the blame, and pretend that everything is okay. This is truly an unfortunate attitude. No humility, no repentance, and no entering the kingdom can occur from this vantage point. Neither we nor they can get through the "eye of the needle" with such pride.

Every now and then, we in our prideful society need to remind ourselves that the sin which caused Satan to fall from heaven was PRIDE. He was an archangel who had a position right next to God. Because of his great beauty and his attributes, he wanted to lift himself above God.(Isaiah 14:11-15) He even led a rebellion in heaven and took a third of the angels with him. That is when he lost his position and was thrown out of heaven.(Revelation 12:9). His beauty and talents which had been given to him by God, caused his pride and his downfall. If we allow the talents our Lord has given to us or our children to lift us up in pride, we are in a very dangerous place indeed. We are operating as Satan did.

In the secret place
of our prayer closet,
we must be honest with God
and with ourselves

So what should we do? We must undertake one of the hardest parts of being a parent. We must seek the path of humility and strip away all pride. In the secret place of our prayer closet, we must be honest with God and with ourselves. When we encounter wrongs in the lives of our children, we must repent for them. Often times the Lord will show us things for which we, as parents, need to repent. It's hard to face the fact that we have not always been perfect parents. But we haven't! No one has. So let's admit the obvious, and be done with it!

One great paradox of God's kingdom is the grace which comes to the humble. When we, as parents, acknowledge our shortcomings and those of our children, an amazing thing happens. We begin to make contact with God's grace in a profound way. He forgives us, refreshes us, and lifts us up. Then we begin to see His plan in action.

James 4:6
God is opposed to the proud, but gives grace to the humble.

James 4:10
Humble yourselves in the presence of the Lord,
and He will exalt you.

We begin to see hearts change. We begin to see actions change. We begin to see more than we even ask for coming to pass. Faith arises like never before!

I pray that you understand the significance of this attitude. If you humble yourself before God and repent for your wrongs, He will honor you in ways that amaze you! You don't want His resistance; you want His grace!

Let's Go Deeper

1. Let the Lord shine His light into your heart.

2. Is there pride?
   Are you too proud to admit the faults
   of your children?

3. Repent and be refreshed.

*And whenever
you stand praying,
forgive,
if you have anything
against anyone
Mark 11:25*

Chapter Fifteen

Are You Ready To Forgive?

When I was going through the "Great War of 2006," (see Introduction) one of my daughters was suffering a grave injustice. Deeds, as well as words, had pummeled her until she was tremendously wounded. I was very angry over the mistreatment. When I tried to pray, I found myself so bitter! The heavens seemed brass.

One day I was agonizing and playing the "tapes of injustice" in my mind. Do you know what I mean? There seem to be tapes that play over and over, reliving the horrendous things which have been done to us. On that particular day, while I was in my misery, the Lord spoke to me and said two words, "Matthew 18." I was startled! Could He be talking to me? I knew what was there; I had taught it many times. It was about forgiveness.

I didn't want to talk about forgiveness! This was different. This was real life. This was MY life! My daughter had suffered grave injustice! Yet if I was going to follow His voice,

I had to do what he said. Obediently, but almost reluctantly, I turned to the chapter and began to read.

Matthew 18: 21-35

Then Peter came and said to Him, "Lord, how often shall my brother sin against me and I forgive him? Up to seven times?"

Jesus said to him, "I do not say to you up to seven times, but up to seventy times seven.

For this reason the Kingdom of Heaven may be compared to a certain king who wished to settle accounts with his slaves.

And when he had begun to settle them, there was brought to him one who owed him ten thousand talents.

But since he did not have the means to repay, his lord commanded him to be sold along with his wife and children and all that he had, and repayment to be made.

The slave therefore falling down, prostrated himself before him, saying, 'Have patience with me, and I will repay you everything.'

And the lord of that slave felt compassion and released him and forgave him the debt.

But that slave went out and found one of his fellow slaves who owed him a hundred denarii; and he seized him and began to choke him, saying, 'Pay back what you owe.'

So his fellow slave fell down and began to entreat him, saying, 'Have patience with me and I will repay you.'

He was unwilling however, but went and threw him in prison until he should pay back what was owed.

So when his fellow slaves saw what had happened, they were deeply grieved and came and reported to their lord all that had happened.

Then summoning him, his lord said to him, 'You wicked slave, I forgave you all that debt because you entreated me.

Should you not also have had mercy on your slave, even as I had mercy on you?'

And his lord, moved with anger, handed him over to the torturers until he should repay all that was owed him.

So shall My Heavenly Father also do to you, if each of you does not forgive his brother from your heart.

In this scripture, Jesus talks about a slave who owed his master a huge sum of money, and his master forgave him the debt. But then this slave went out and showed no mercy toward a slave who owed him just a little. It's obvious that Jesus is comparing this master and slave to Himself and us. He has forgiven us so much. We had no ability to pay for our sinful nature, and all the mistakes we have made. Yet our Lord willingly forgave us. Then when we go out and hold others' sins against them, we are acting as the wicked slave.

I had taught that passage so many times over the years: forgive always and never hold onto anger. Yet there I was, harboring resentment. When you are in the middle of a crisis, it's so easy to slip. You may have knowledge of what to do, but in the middle of the battle the atmosphere can get very cloudy. You can't see as well.

Forgiveness is not an option, It's a requirement

That day I got very still and began to praise my God. I read from Psalms and prayed. As the clouds lifted, I forgave. There were many tears, but I forgave anyway. Then sitting in the stillness, alone with my God, that wonderful fresh oil from heaven poured upon me. Sweet peace. I knew that my Father was at work on my behalf.

Whatever you are going through, forgiveness is not an option. It is a requirement. Perhaps unfair treatment, false accusations, or outright viciousness are swirling around. You may have to deal with the perpetrators in an open and direct way. Yet you still have to forgive them, knowing that your Father will take care of you. He is the Judge, not you. He will work on your behalf only when you operate according to His rules. Bitterness and anger have to be relinquished if you expect your Father to work on your behalf.

Let's see more of what Jesus had to say about it.

Read Matthew 6:14-15

Just after telling people how to pray, Jesus says:
For if you forgive men their transgressions, your heavenly Father will also forgive you.
But if you do not forgive men, then your Father will not forgive your transgressions.

Now read Mark 11:22-24

Have Faith in God

Truly I say to you, whoever says to this mountain, "Be taken up and cast into the sea, and does not doubt in his heart, but believes that what he says is going to happen, it shall be granted him. Therefore I say to you, all things for which you pray and ask, believe that you have received them, and they shall be granted you.

Wow! We've talked about these verses before. Don't we love them? Power and more power! Mountain-moving faith!

But wait. There's more. Let's read on. Uh-oh! Look what it says.

> Mark 11:25-26
>
> *And whenever you stand praying, forgive, if you have*
> *anything against anyone; so that your Father also who*
> *is in heaven may forgive you your transgressions.*
>
> *(But if you do not forgive, neither will your Father*
> *who is in heaven forgive your transgressions).*

This sounds serious, doesn't it? Well, it is! Jesus made it clear over and over that you and I have to forgive others if we expect to be walking in that covenant with God. He even says if you have "anything against anyone" you must forgive them. There doesn't seem to be much wiggle room in that one. We want to be in covenant with our God. We want Him to hear our prayers and take us down that path of deliverance for our children. It's obvious: We Must Forgive!!

There will be times when the only way you can forgive is to allow the Holy Spirit to give you that ability. It may require tremendous faith. But He is more than willing and able to empower you in this way.

As you forgive – however hard it may be, you will see God's handiwork like never before. The heavens will open up. You will know in your heart that your answer is on the way.

Let's Go Deeper

Right now spend some time with God. You might take communion and rededicate your life. Praise Him. Ask Him to shine His light into your heart. Are you harboring unforgiveness? Be honest. He knows anyway. Just admit it to Him as you worship Him alone. That Babylonian garment is just not worth the price.

Is there anyone you need to forgive? I know. They don't deserve it. Neither do I. Neither do you. The Lord has been leading us into a greater understanding of His plan of prayer. But only clean hands and a pure heart are allowed on this mountain. It's a beautiful place to be. Don't let anything keep you from going up!

An excellent wife,
who can find?
For her worth
is far
above jewels
Proverbs 31:10

Chapter Sixteen
Woman Of Power

We have hit upon a lot of topics in this book. I hope that you are feeling that your prayer skills have been honed, and that you have been inspired to pray more. Throughout the Word there are scriptures which will speak to you and give you greater wisdom in prayer. When your eyes are opened to see, you see wisdom everywhere!

Proverbs 31 is an example of that.

Proverbs 31: 10-11

An excellent wife, who can find?
Her worth is far above jewels.
The heart of her husband trusts in her and she has no
lack of gain.
She does him good and not evil all the days of her life.

Every woman of God wants to be the Proverbs 31 woman. She is strong, faithful, productive, admired, and loved. You might say that she is a woman of power!

Earlier as we talked about logos and rhema, we mentioned how words can suddenly leap off the page and speak to you profoundly. Remember? That is what happened to me concerning Proverbs 31. As I was reading and meditating on these scriptures one day, the Lord really opened my eyes! "Why that woman is a prayer warrior," I thought! I got so excited seeing the depth of meaning. I want to share some of it with you.

Now I know that these verses are speaking of natural things, like productivity and diligence. However, let's look for the hidden meanings. You'll love seeing it this way, just like I do!

She is ready to appropriate all that Heaven has to offer

These are the ones I call the intercessory prayer verses:

Proverbs 31: 13-21

She looks for wool and flax ,
And works with her hands in delight.

The wool and flax represent the "covering" for her family. Often prayer is considered a "covering." When people are covered in prayer they are under the umbrella of God. The angels are looking after them. The demons don't have easy access. There is generally protection and favor.

She is like merchant ships
And brings her food from afar.

By drawing from the Spirit within her and by drawing on the Word, this woman of prayer is not settling for just what might happen from day to day. She is full of energy and vigor. She is ready to appropriate all that heaven has to offer. She might have to dig into the Word to bring that food from afar, but she is determined to get it. She is determined to bring that perfect will into her life and into the lives of her family by going into her prayer closet to appropriate God's best.

She rises also while it is still night
And gives food to her household,
And portions to her maidens.

It's easy to believe God's promises when we have them in our hand. When your prayer has just been answered, of course you believe! But what if things look bleak? What if it is still "night?" Will you rise up, take dominion, and rule even before you see daylight? Will you believe God for a miracle breakthrough when your son is still on drugs? When your daughter is rebellious? When your husband seems indifferent? Will you rise up while it is still night and start giving assignments – even to the angels - your servants?

She considers a field and buys it;
From her earnings she plants a vineyard.

This is my favorite verse in the entire proverb, because of a special experience I had with the Lord. One day many years ago I was spending some time in fasting and prayer. I was reading the Bible and "just happened" to be in the 13th chapter of Matthew. I read

Matthew 13:44

The kingdom of heaven is like a treasure hidden in the field,
which a man found and hid, and from joy over it, he goes and
sells all that he has, and buys that field.

That is a verse you and I have read many times. I had always thought of a pot of gold or a treasure chest filled with gold buried in the middle of a field. Have you ever had that picture? Well, on that particular day just as I read that verse, I had a little vision. It was just a flash, but it was clear.

I saw a plot of farmland. It was about an acre of freshly plowed and planted soil. Since I live in an agricultural area, it was a very familiar sight. There were many rows – very neat. Rows and rows of fresh dirt. I knew that the field had been freshly planted with seed. There was not any green in sight. Only fresh dirt. It was planted with no evidence of the crop it would yield.

Suddenly I knew what the Father was saying. The treasure was the Word of God, His seed. The man found the treasure in the Bible as he read it and planted it diligently in his field. (The first planting had to be in the man's heart, but then he began to plant the word into the atmosphere of the spirit realm: he decreed it.) There was nothing that could be seen with the human eye. By faith he knew that he had been planting it, and he knew it was there.

God's Word is like treasure hidden in a field

The farmer came to a place where he treasured what he was planting so much, that he was willing to "sell" or "give up" all the other preconceived ideas. He was willing to give up believing what his eyes were telling him (His eyes were telling him there was nothing there. His eyes only saw what looked like bare soil). But he knew what was planted and that is what he was buying! He was buying that field full of the treasure of the Word of God.

Let me give an example. Let's say your grandson is an alcoholic. Everyone has talked to him and told him he shouldn't drink. But he has his own mind, and he continues to drink. He gets a couple of DUI's, but that doesn't seem to phase him. He still continues to drink.

You, on the other hand, start seeing in the Word that your grandchildren are blessed because of you. You see where your God promised that "He would circumcise your heart and the hearts of your children and your grandchildren so they could love Him and live!" (Deuteronomy 30:6) You begin to plant that seed in the field of your heart – and you speak it out into the atmosphere of the spirit. You decree it! You are hiding treasure in the field.

You have joy because of what you know is in that field

Now you begin to have joy because of what you know is in that field. Others will come to you and say, "There is no hope for that boy! He's hopeless. Don't even think that he will get any better. He'll never turn around." But you "sell," or give up, those comments. You buy the field with everything that is within you. You know that even though you don't see a sprig of green now, you will! You are operating in the kingdom of Heaven.

Now let's take another look at the proverb.

Proverbs 31:16
She considers a field and buys it.
With her earnings she plants a vineyard.

Do you now see which field she is considering? It's the field planted with the treasure of God's Word. The woman of prayer buys that field every time! Then the earnings from that field are producing on their own. The son, the daughter, or the grandchild you are praying for rises up out of the dust and begins to produce. Your "earnings" are the people who have been delivered through your prayer. And they will begin to produce. Thus, a vineyard is planted! What productivity! That is what you can expect as you continue in your prayer.

The next few verses talk about strength and determination – all of which are so essential to your success in prayer. We have to see the vision, gird ourselves with strength, not let our lamps go out – even at night, and get the job done!

Proverbs 31:21 is another favorite.

She is not afraid of the snow for her household
For all her household are clothed in scarlet.

Do you remember earlier in the book we talked about the word being rain and snow?

Remember Psalm 147:15-19

He sends forth His command to the earth
His Word runs very swiftly .
He gives snow like wool;
He scatters the frost like ashes.
He casts forth His ice as fragments;
Who can stand before His cold?
He sends forth His Word and melts them;
He causes His wind to blow and waters to flow.
He declares His Word to Jacob, His statutes and ordinances to
Israel.

The snow represents the Word of the Bible when it is not understood. It seems to be locked up; it's frozen. It hasn't been revealed. The Pharisees knew what the Word said, but they couldn't understand it. That is why they always attacked Jesus.

Very often when people are praying for their children, they begin to get discouraged. They think, "Joey just doesn't get it! He acts so foolisly. He doesn't seem to realize what he is doing." That is when they are dealing with snow in the lives of their children, and not running water. The Word is frozen so that their loved ones can't understand it. They don't seem to see it.

But the woman dedicated to prayer and to her Maker, isn't afraid of the snow. She isn't afraid that the Word will be locked up from her household. She knows that those of her household are "clothed in scarlet." They are covered by the blood of Jesus because of her covenant. The Word won't stay in the form of snow. In due time, it will melt. The rhema word will come. The waters will flow and her loved ones will be able to hear the voice of God. They will once again be able to walk with their God.

Proverbs 31:28-29

Her children rise up and bless her;
Her husband also, and he praises her saying
Many daughters have done nobly
But you excel them all.

Be strong. Stand firm. Don't give up. And the time will come when you will see your children RISE UP. They will lift their eyes to heaven and call upon their God. They will receive their inheritance of forgiveness and deliverance. At that time they will call you blessed. They will appreciate your diligence on their behalf. Your husband also will honor your spirituality. So keep it up!

Over the years, I have been amazed at the number of verses the Lord has "quickened," or revealed, to me as prayer verses. Just as in the case of this proverb, there may a natural understanding also. But He always seems to have hidden meanings which He wants to show us: meanings which will bring us into a greater fullness of His plan.

As you read the Word, ask the Holy Spirit to give you more insight. He wants to. Just ask Him and then listen for His answers. He will give you tremendous understanding as you continue.

Let's Go Deeper

Read Proverbs 31: 10-31

Write down some of the insights which especially
encourage you in your prayer life.

The righteous man
will flourish
like the palm tree;
He will grow
like a cedar
in Lebanon
Psalms 92:12

The Journey
Continues

L ife goes on. The journey continues. There is always more to learn and more to do. There is al-
ways a closer walk with our Father available. There is always a
higher mark He beckons us to reach.

The prayer examples in this book were of children who
were in dire situations. Yet God's perfect plan is not to wait
until there is a problem. When life is running along smoothly
we still need to pray for our children. We need to pray when
things are good and pray when things are bad. In that way we
are able to truly cover our offspring with God's greatest mercy
and favor.

So we are on the path of God which is forever upward. We walk that path with patience, perseverance, and joy.
We embrace our future and the future of our families. We are
making a difference. Our children are making a difference also.
Our vineyard will be great!

My prayer is that you will feel more confident in your ability to pray. It seems that when understanding is there, prayer is just a natural outflow of your life with your Maker.

You may be wishing that I would give you some prayers for you to pray. But I want you to pray your own prayers. Start with your relationship and communication with your Father and His Word. Trust Him to show you what to pray for, what to say, when to pray. He will also guide you into deeper understanding of prayer and give you greater faith in your ability to do it.

So don't give up. Never let circumstances stop you from moving forward. Those circumstances can change. God's Word never changes. God's Word has the power to change everything around us.

Your future is bright. So embrace it. And embrace your God. Your life is a journey. With God, it's a heavenly journey; a journey which leads

Forever Upward!

Forever,
O Lord,
Thy Word
is settled
in heaven
Psalms 119:89

Scripture Prayers and Promises

For A Deeper Walk

Deuteronomy 28:13

And the Lord shall make you the head and not the tail, and you only shall be above, and you shall not be underneath, if you will listen to the commandments of the Lord your God, which I charge you today, to observe them carefully.

Psalm 1:1-3

How blessed is the man who does not walk in the counsel of the wicked, nor stand in the path of sinners, nor sit in the seat of scoffers.

But his delight is in the law of the Lord, and in His law he meditates day and night,

And he will be like a tree firmly planted by streams of water, which yields its fruit in its season

And its leaf does not wither, and in whatever he does he prospers.

Psalm 91:1

He who dwells in the shelter of the Most High will abide under the shadow of the Almighty.

Psalm 91: 11-16

For He will give His angels charge concerning you, to
guard you in all your ways;
They will bear you up in their hands lest you strike
your foot against a stone.
You will tread upon the lion and cobra, the young lion
and the serpent you will trample down.
Because he has loved Me, therefore I will deliver him.
I will be with him in trouble;
I will rescue him and honor him
With long life I will satisfy him,
And let him behold my salvation.

Isaiah 53:5

But he was pierced through for our transgressions,
He was crushed for our iniquities;
The chastening for our well-being fell upon Him,
And by His scourging we are healed.

Isaiah 54:14

In righteousness you will be established;
You will be far from oppression, for you will not fear;
And from terror, for it will not come near you.

Isaiah 54:17

No weapon that is formed against you shall prosper;
And every tongue that accuses you in judgment you
will condemn.
This is the heritage of the servants of the Lord,
And their vindication is from me, declares the Lord.

Ephesians 1: 16-19

I do not cease giving thanks for you while making mention of you in my prayers that the God of our Lord Jesus Christ, The Father of glory, may give to you a spirit of wisdom and revelation in the knowledge of Him

I pray that the eyes of your heart may be enlightened, so that you may know what is the hope of His calling, what are the riches of the glory of His inheritance in the saints, and what is the surpassing greatness of His power toward us who believe.

Ephesians 3: 14-21

For this reason I bow my knees before the Father, from whom every family in heaven and on earth derives its name, that He would grant you, according to the riches of His glory, to be strengthened with power through His Spirit in the inner man

so that Christ may dwell in your hearts through faith; and that you, being rooted and grounded in love, may be able to comprehend with all the saints what is the breadth and length and height and depth,

and to know the love of Christ which surpasses knowledge, that you may be filled up to all the fulness of God.

Now to Him who is able to do exceeding abundantly beyond all that we ask or think, according to the power that works within us,

To Him be the glory in the church and in Christ Jesus to all generations forever and ever. Amen.

Colossians 1:9-12

For this reason also, since the day we heard of it, we have not ceased to pray for you and to ask that you may be filled with the knowledge of His will in all spiritual wisdom and understanding,

So that you may walk in a manner worthy of the Lord, to please Him in all respects, bearing fruit in every good work and increasing in the knowledge of God;

strengthened with all power, according to His glorious might, for the attaining of all steadfastness and patience,

joyously giving thanks to the Father , who has qualified us to share in the inheritance of the saints in light.

I John 4:4

You are from God, little children, and have overcome them; because greater is He who is in you than he who is in the world.

For Husbands

Genesis 2:24

For this cause a man shall leave his father and his mother, and shall cleave to his wife; and they shall become one flesh.

Proverbs 5:18

Let your fountain be blessed and rejoice in the wife of your youth.

Proverbs 21:1

> The king's heart is like channels of water in the hand
> of the Lord;
> He turns it wherever He wishes.

Proverbs 31:28

> Her children rise up and bless her;
> Her husband also, and he praises her.

Ephesians 5:22-23; 25

> Wives, be subject to your own husbands, as to the
> Lord. For the husband is head of the wife as Christ is
> head of the church, He himself being the Savior of
> the body.
> Husbands, love your wives, just as Christ also loved
> the church and gave Himself up for her.

Romans 15:5-7

> Now may the God who gives perseverance and en-
> couragement grant you to be of the same mind with
> one another according to Christ Jesus that with one
> accord you may, with one voice, glorify the God and
> Father of our Lord Jesus Christ. Wherefore accept one
> another, just as Christ also accepted us to the glory of
> God.

For Children

Deuteronomy 28:4a

> Blessed shall be the offspring of your body.

Deuteronomy 30:6

> Moreover the Lord your God will circumcise your
> heart and the heart of your descendants, to love the

Lord your God with all your heart and with all your soul, in order that you may live.

Psalm 112:2

Praise the Lord! How blessed is the man who fears the Lord, who greatly delights in His commandments.
His descendents shall be mighty upon the earth. The generation of the upright will be blessed.

Proverbs 11:21

Assuredly, the evil man will not go unpunished,
But the descendants of the righteous will be delivered.

Isaiah 44:3

For I will pour out water on the thirsty land and streams on the dry ground.
I will pour out My Spirit on your offspring and My blessing on your descendants.

Isaiah 54:13

And all your sons will be taught of the Lord;
And the well-being of your sons will be great.

Isaiah 59:21

And as for Me, this is My covenant with them, says the Lord: "My Spirit which is upon you, and My words which I have put in your mouth, shall not depart from your mouth, nor from the mouth of your offspring, nor from the mouth of your offspring's offspring," says the Lord, from now and forever.

Isaiah 61:9

Then their offspring will be known among the nations, and their descendants in the midst of the peoples. All who see them will recognize them because they are the offspring whom the Lord has blessed.

Jeremiah 31:16-17

Thus says the Lord,
"Restrain your voice from weeping,
And your eyes from tears;
For your work shall be rewarded," declares the Lord
"And they shall return from the land of the enemy.
And there is hope for your future," declares the Lord.
"And your children shall return to their own territory."

Ephesians 6:1-4

Children, obey your parents in the Lord, for this is right. Honor your father and mother (which is the first commandment with a promise), that it may be well with you, and that you may live long on the earth.

And fathers, do not provoke your children to anger; but bring them up in the discipline and instruction of the Lord.

Be Strong and Courageous

Psalm 138:8

The Lord will accomplish what concerns me;
Thy lovingkindness, O Lord, is everlasting;
Do not forsake the works of your hands.

Habakkuk 3:17-19

Though the fig tree should not blossom
And there be no fruit on the vine
Though the yield of the olive should fail
And the fields produce no food.
Though the flock should be cut off from the fold,
And there be no cattle in the stalls.
Yet I will exult in the Lord,
I will rejoice in the God of my salvation.
The Lord God is my strength.
And He has made my feet like hinds' feet,
And makes me walk on my high places.

Jeremiah 33:10-11

Thus says the Lord, "Yet again there shall be heard in this place, of which you say, 'It is a waste, without man and without beast,' that is, in the cities of Judah and in the streets of Jerusalem that are desolate without man and without inhabitant and without beast,

the voice of joy and the voice of gladness, the voice of the bridegroom and the voice of the bride, the voice of those who say,

'Give thanks to the Lord of hosts,
For the Lord is good,
For His lovingkindness is everlasting.'
and of those who bring a thank offering into the house of

the Lord. For I will restore the fortunes of the land as they were at first." says the Lord

II Corinthians 10:3-5

For though we walk in the flesh, we do not war according to the flesh,

For the weapons of our warfare are not of the flesh, but divinely powerful for the destruction of fortresses.

We are destroying speculations and every lofty thing raised up against the knowledge of God, and we are taking every thought captive to the obedience of Christ.

Ephesians 6:10

Finally, be strong in the Lord and in the strength of His might.

Hebrews 6:10-12

For God is not unjust so as to forget your work and the love which you have shown toward His name, in having ministered and in still ministering to the saints.

And we desire that each one of you show the same diligence so as to realize the full assurance of hope until the end,

that you may not be sluggish, but through faith and patience inherit the promises.

The Word is full of scriptures which will speak to you, building your faith and confidence. I have shared some which are special to me. You will want to find others and put them in your hearts.

It takes time in prayer and time with God to collect your verses which are so special to you. But it is worth the effort. Your verses will be more significant to you than mine are.

As always, the main thing is to do it!

About The Author

Suellen Estes had a very dramatic encounter with Jesus in September, 1979. During early adulthood, intellectualism had driven her away from her Savior. As she met Him really for the first time, her life changed forever. Soon after, Suellen received the baptism in the Holy Spirit and a tremendous hunger for God's Word.

Since that time, Suellen has had a desire to share with others the awesome power of God's love. Her speaking engagements and seminars focus on helping others to grow in their ability to connect with God and partake of that love for themselves.

A mother of four children and a grandmother of nine, Suellen often ministers to mothers and fathers concerning their children. Her teaching encourages parents to pursue God's promises in His Word and to stand in prayer until those promises are manifested in the earth.

Suellen assists her husband, Mickey, as they pastor

Life Connection Church
Blue Mountain, Mississippi
www.lifeconnection.ms

Feel free to contact Suellen at
www.foreverupward.com
suellen@foreverupward.com
She would like to hear from you.

beauty
things

zestivia